T0309676

Michel Serres

Biogea

Biogée by Michel Serres
© editions-dialogue.fr/Le Pommier 2010

Translated by Randolph Burks
as *Biogea*

First Edition
Minneapolis © 2012, Univocal Publishing

Published by Univocal
123 North 3rd Street, #202
Minneapolis, MN 55401

Designed & Printed by Jason Wagner
Distributed by the University of Minnesota Press

ISBN 9781937561086
Library of Congress Control Number 2012937744

Contents

1   Sea and River

27   Earth and Mountains

53   Three Volcanoes

81   Winds and
         Atmospheric Phenomena

95   Flora and Fauna

135   Encounters, Loves

For Beatrice,
A guide in the life and the Earth sciences.

My soul today is becoming a tree. Yesterday, I felt it to be a spring. Tomorrow?… Will I rise with the smoke of an altar, or will I hold the altitude above the plains, with the feeling of power of the vulture on its slow wings; do I know it?

Paul Valery, *Dialogue de l'arbre* [Dialogue of the Tree] Œ*uvres*, II, Pléiade, p. 178

… for forests, hills, fire and water alone have voices, speak a language. We've lost the secret of it, although the memory of an august accord, of the ineffable alliance of intelligence and things, cannot be forgotten even by the lowliest. The voice that we no longer understand is still friendly, fraternal, a maker of serene peace.

George Bernanos, *L'Imposture* [The Imposter]
Pléiade, p. 326

Sea and River

We made fun of him, old Taciturn; we thought he was cracked, driven crazy by strange mania. "Danger is near," he would mutter into a beard he kept short; we used to laugh paying no heed to his prophecies, which were the result, we thought, of premature senility and also a lot of disgust for the present day that grumblers of a certain age like to proclaim. And he used to set off traveling, sometimes without saying where he was going; he would always come back more preoccupied.

Worse, one day we saw him buy, at the pit sawyer's, beautiful arched beams that he set up in his farmyard as a kind of inverted framework, with the beam of the frame being quite wide and solidly jointed. Thin, skillful, always bent over hammer or pincers, he worked on it for months. The neighbors would hear the muffled blows of his mallet on the wooden dowels that held the mortise and tenons. Little by little, it took on the look of a boat whose square walls, pierced with scuttles, could pass for those of a house. "A boat on land, a ship in the sink," we would sing. From time to time, he would transport tools on board, some livestock from his barn, even wild animals in cages and items of furniture. My word, this stubborn mule was moving out!

Since I ranked among his kin, one day he invited me to follow him on one of his peregrinations. It should be said that our hamlets were scattered over an immense plain shaped like a basin – round, low, deep – whose fertile soil and mild climate produced various vegetables and fruits; especially cherries, so famous all around that we made a fortune selling them by the cartload or, with honey, in jellies. Yes, a certain material comfort reigned there, and we didn't understand Taciturn's worries. So we left, the two of us, one morning, heading due south, and for several days we had to climb endless twists and turns along a high hill that led, after sixteen nights under the stars, to the shores of the sea. Not a word had surmounted the barrier of his teeth.

Arrived there, "Listen," he said. I didn't hear anything except the murmur of the wind above the short swell and the cries of a few seagulls, nothing else. Dazzled, I had never seen the ocean before. Sand, beach, seaweed, desert. "Listen more closely," he insisted. And, indeed, in the depths of the Earth, beneath my feet, I thought I heard a muffled roaring, like an irregular rumbling, a kind of low thunder that made the ground shake like a wave. I even began to feel its vibration beneath the soles of my feet. I questioned the Old Man with my eyes.

He watched the open sea for a long while. "An interminable history," he continued. The family elders heard it from distant forebears who heard it from even more remote ancestors and so on, a Grand Narrative to which many of us didn't lend any credence and which recounted that, in the past, there hadn't been any water there. Only a black hole, a bottomless cavity, an unfathomable cavern. One might have thought the opening of the Underworld. Yet, however far they were going, travelers could voyage for thousands of leagues along the rim of this enormous ditch; in a year on a horse at least, you might nonetheless travel around it, punctuated now and again, on the vertiginous heights, by wide cataracts through which the waters of several rivers would rush, rivers whose estuaries or deltas mark, today, the locations of these cascades.

"Older if that is possible, other idle tales also claimed that in even more distant times, the sea had, like today, already invaded this void. That it would dry up, that it would fill up again, I tell you in rhythms of tens of thousands of years. That this fluctuation depended on those earthquakes whose terror you've often felt and which either closed the pit or, on the contrary, opened it to the immense ocean that surrounds the Earth through the columns located to the far west of us." Taciturn then stretched his arm toward the setting sun. "The blows of the quakes either broke its dikes or obstructed them, accordingly. So the waters entered our oblong pit surrounded by the inhabited lands in torrents; conversely, at the end of several times a thousand years, they evaporated, and everything became blue-green and black again."

He turned around, with his back to the sea. Our homeland stretched to the horizon in front of us, a broad, cheerful and hollow dome. As far as the eye could see, plowed fields, cherry orchards, meadows for sheep, adobe structures for families, metal sheds for tools, wooden barns for livestock. "A happy country, isn't it?" he said. I gave my approval with my brow. "To enjoy such a view here, you see that we're perched on the ridge of a kind of partition, on a thin and long crest that protects our basin from the waters of the sea. What would happen if it broke?"

"Now, ever since my youth, my grandfather often took me here and told me that his great grandfather had told him that, ever since his youth, the water had been rising. Yes, for as long as the family memory has been passed on, its level has been continuously rising. Measure it, beneath your feet; the sea now reaches to the brim."

"I had you come for a second reason. There is a new one: an event that none of these old traditions tell of, taking place for some months. That noise you hear, you might think, wouldn't you, that it's a rumbling similar to the beginnings of an earthquake. Never spoken of, nor heard; nothing about it in any narrative. Yet listen, listen to it well. I've been listening to it for seven years. You hear it too, I see. It hasn't stopped growing since I've been coming here. What is it saying? Does it have some meaning? Who is speaking? Can we understand its warning? Will I one day be able to decipher this call from the Earth? Listen to its voice. Our Earth is speaking, you feel it; it's recounting something to us, the way your mother did, evenings, when you weren't able to get to sleep; it's saying what it knows. What? Who is it speaking to? I've been studying it for ages, this voice, I don't dare speak about it to anyone since, in the village, everyone takes me for a fool, a visionary, a mystic, a bad citizen who takes no interest in political affairs."

"Nevertheless here is my translation of the rumbling: it's announcing that the wall is cracking and is going to collapse, yes, the one on which, uneasy, we're perched. I have a feeling its panel is going to fall down. Without knowing it, we're living, we stockbreeders or farmers, in the navel of a great cavity defended by a screen so thin and strained that it threatens to burst under the pressure of the water. It'll crack. On that day of wrath, the sea of the middle of the earth will invade our basin, will fill the sacred earth of the ancestors. Quickly, to the evacuation points! That's why, with my trembling old man's hands, I'm attempting to build a boat. A madman's ship on dry land. And I'm stacking up in its holds, as in a strong box, everything that could be of use in the event of danger. As for the Rest, every man for himself!"

"But no one listens to me. Everyone is fascinated by interesting disputes, tragic quarrels between people, villages and hamlets, by conflicts between petty leaders and their permanent theater. They don't know what they're doing; they love violence so much that it increases like a flood that's always ready to cover the entire Earth. Will they also understand that, some day?" He accented this word with a citation of his heel. I didn't mention that we were walking bare foot.

About what hidden knowledge was this madman who had the appearance of a wise man holding forth? I listened to his wild yarn with a well-raised child's courteousness. Taking our time and regaining silence once again, we went back down to the village. Over long months, he no longer spoke to me, stricken by the melancholy that I neither believed in nor understood the predictions he claimed were scientific.

Right up until the morning when – with a sudden cry whose splitting intensity increased in frequency to the top of the scale and which all at once occupied the entire expanse of celestial space above the basin – everything cracked. And the water came, from the left, from the right, in high waves, at ground level, in cataracts and rushing tides, like a tsunami. The mountain partition had just given way. Splashing about amid the whirlpools of a flaming current and almost drowning in the viscous mud, I then hurtled down, luckily, not far from his baroque structure, oval and square. Who felt like laughing at it on this day? At the end of a boat hook, he held a hawser out to me and, hanging on the hook, I climbed aboard, among the calves, cows, pigs and broods. Around him was his little family of beasts, stupefied, – each of them going about with its chirping or terror-stricken baying – potted flowers, spilt seeds, scythes, pitchforks, yokes hanging from hooks.

We sailed forty days, worried, tossed about on board in a thick fog, up until a relative drop in the water level. The boat's keel touched bottom then on the flanks of Mt. Ararat, amid the doves and olive trees. There was nobody left, villagers or peasants, a human silence and desert. Beneath the returned sun, port of us, extended the calm weather of that immense pool that would later be called the Black Sea, at the bottom of which have slumbered, ever since, my drowned forebears and my country, villages, cabins and plowed fields, beneath the furrows of which sleep, still today, even more deeply, enormous tectonic tensions.

Two memories culminate this adventure, ancient: the deafening noise of the break at its beginning and the dazzling rainbow on the last day of the flood, the first where we made peace with the world.

The numerous legends from which I drew this narrative, amusingly putting my own image in it, recount, in various languages, that upon landing old Taciturn planted vines, no doubt Noah's plants, and that – seasons gone by, grape harvests done, wine tapped – he got drunk on joy; or brewed beer and did the same with that. These fermented drinks saved this remainder of humanity from the bad waters; the artificial paradise of biotechnology emerged from this hellish deluge.

Under a new sky and in a steady breeze, this group who escaped catastrophe was born, new, from the cruel mother sea. First rebirth.

Hymn to the Sea Paradise

I have nevertheless lived the paradise of the waters. Yes, I have inhabited the sea, I have frequented the high seas, just as uninhabitable as the high mountains, pack ice, or the desert. Everywhere else, habitation remains possible; but in these high inhospitable places the planet, inhuman, reveals itself. Nevertheless, when I lost the sea, on land, things became lackluster. The sea and I used to vibrate with joy.

At the end of our meals on the sea, we would be growing impatient with dessert when, invariably, one of us, abandoning the fruit, would cry out: "How about going out to see the sea?" In the time it took to eat lunch we already missed her, whereas sailing, we hardly ever left her. More than for bread or wine – in love, passionate, mystic – we were hungry and thirsty for her. As our horizon, we had the sea. As our mistress, we had the sea. As our goddess, we had the sea. As our house, the sea. As our path, garden, hammock and table, the sea. As our love, the sea. Pitching and rolling, paradise, a dance in aperiodic rhythm of lovers and beloved combined. We had the sea as our friend....

... but as our enemy, the sea, all the more beloved because her triumphant fury made us tremble, the devastating sea, indifferent to our suffering like a cruel mistress, the sea that could suddenly present itself before the bow like a high and unique cliff or mountain face collapsing, shattered, over the quickwork like a tsunami, the sea that sometimes forced us to stand, upright, on the cabin or bridge walls while the floor turned vertical, the sea terror that haunted the nights of insomnia beneath the hooting of the foghorn, the abominable sea, wife and daughter of the breeze, passive before the wind, the sea that swept away the tackle and swallowed lives, the deadly sea....

... the living sea, vital, vivifying, first mother of the living species, the maternal sea, soft as a baby's skin, without a ripple, rocked in the calm after the storm, flowering breast, uterus, fertile womb, generous source of fecundity, parturient and nourishing to the point of repletion, multiply populated with monsters and marvels whose forms made us toss and turn at night in our bunks, clawed by the nightmares of the deep, the primeval Eve sea from whose wombs we all came, seaweed, plants and animals, bacteria and mammals, reptiles and whales, even humans, billions, then millions of years ago....

... the sea soiled by hoodlums, violators of their first mother – quick, let squadrons of pirates rise up and embark with me to stop and examine these matricidal polluters, to seize them and throw them, naked, into dungeons – the seas, victims and soon to be dead, who will defend them except the sailors....

... the beautiful woman sea, open vulva, dear mother, tender lover, lovable sister, a pretty girl unpredictable in her whims, a fearsome, fickle mistress, a cruel mother whose head bristles with snakes, a sorceress enchantress, producer of love and despair potions.

On land, the rest of my dull hours from then on found their only recompense in nostalgia for this transcendent lover, in whose vagina, curled up, I used to live, sleep, think, inhabit. I still carry her in me like a drowned romance.

Yes, I mourn for the sea whose demanding beauty outmatches that of my words, all too human. And I forget the beauty of lives. Life at sea quickly attains the status of a work of art because inhabiting that part of the uninhabitable Biogea requires a reversal of the body and soul that can convert the sailor to the divine. I remember twilights during which, standing on the deck sextant in hand, I would be waiting for a star to light up to take a bearing. It sometimes happened then that my attentive gaze immediately changed into that of the sea itself, whose unique eye, a green spherical abyss, was contemplating, ecstatic in its bitter tears, the blue ubiquity, the black presence of the divine.

I was seeing like the sea.

Flood

I became an ocean sailor to get the better of my father, the bargeman. Let me recount the fresh water tales of my youth.

The *longueil* and the *traversier*, these are the names of the two cables that, wound on four winches called the *papillonnage*, tied our dredger, right and left, to the two shores of Garonne. For seen from a plane, the four steel cables, the first two of which, in front, opposed the current while the two at the stern stabilized the pontoon, must have formed the edges of a transparent butterfly covering the width of the river with its spread wings. Not only has my old trade of being a freshwater forced-labor convict – fishing sand, breaking rocks, compacting roads – vanished, but I bemoan the silence of some fifty words I only used with ten bargemen, my father and brother, all vanished: thus speaking this mute language all alone, I ruminate over a dialogue of the dead.

Practical in normal times, this four-cabled mechanism became dangerous during floods because, obstructing the river's width, it intercepted the heaps swept along by the inundation. Suddenly, from the invaded plain and flooded farms the deluge uprooted tree trunks, stumps, entangled bushes, carried furniture away from houses, sometimes framework taken from destroyed roofs, animal corpses, sometimes survivors ... an entire floating and swept-along *bagass*é that we, balanced on our fragile *sapinous*, had to prune with an ax so that the pieces, caught astride the cable would slide off and speed along with the current. They formed cataracts whose strength threatened to rip out our moorings.

Aboard, there were never more than four or five of us keeping watch: the boss, tall and thin, with a small mustache, prominent cheekbones, his two sons, quasi-twins, the dredger, stocky, strong, with his cap constantly pulled down over his baldness, and sometimes his apprentice. Everyone dressed in overalls. I particularly remember our silence and the noise whose pregnance often prevented us from hearing each other and which, since, has never left my ears; the tinnitus I'm permanently afflicted with reproduces with high fidelity the whistling and silky sound of the implacable mass of moving water that, overflowing its regular bed, was then occupying the flood plain, kilometers-wide between the hills called, like us, the Serres. At least my sense of hearing has never left Garonne.

There were, indeed, no more than four or five of us to cut loose the *bagassé*, plug the leaks in the dredger which might be ripped open by the heavy impacts from the stumps and beams, but above all continuously watch over the winches following the height of the low water level. Occasionally, plunged in that intense rumbling and sometimes blinded by the fog, we no longer knew our position very well; lost, it was nonetheless necessary to stay in the low-water channel, for a sudden retreat on the part of the flood would have deposited our flat-bottomed and high-belfried old pontoon boat forever among the apple trees. Without detaching any cable, we had to keep them under tension. Give them slack and take it in again, depending; tie them again to some willow or some more solid mooring. They mustn't break, either, under the weight of the *bagassé*, on pain of letting us slide downstream in the flaming current, helpless. Standing up to the force of the water, fighting against the debris it was bringing, saving what could be saved, boats, tools and persons: for how long? That depended on the bad will of that bitch of a Garonne.

Clinging to planks or scattered beams, sometimes unfortunate people appeared, surprised by the water, engendered before us from the fog, people born from Garonne; when – sculling – we could stem the current, we'd pluck them like plums and hoist them aboard our *gabarrots*. One day around noon, in the very middle of the river, in the most inflamed section of the rapids, an entire haystack went by, the type that farmers in the past would pile up during the harvest for animal litters, on top of which a peasant, hunting rifle in hand, was shooting off salvos to call for help. Turning and rolling amid the eddies, the fragile pile, close to coming undone, glided before our eyes at an insane speed, uncatchable, continued downstream and shattered on the archways of the Pont de Pierre, whose light was blinded by the rise of the waters. Decapitated, the poor wretch? We never did learn. Drowned, surely.

Day and night without interruption, our watch on the river lasted as long as the flood. Sometimes three days, sometimes a week or more. We'd sleep in turns down in the hold, on the sheet metal sole. We didn't always bring enough food. Bread that quickly went stale, ham, Cantal cheese, harsh red wine. The work would warm us up, as well as a brazier with holes, well-stocked with charcoal. We always came back safe and sound, exhausted, famished, black with smoke, stinking filthy, bearded, hands bloodied from having handled so much the ax and prickly cables, disembarked from hell, wild-eyed, proud.

Since neither bank nor shore existed any longer, it was impossible to land. Hardly a few kilometers from our house, itself flooded, we used to find ourselves isolated in the middle of Garonne, as though we were sailing on the other side of the Atlantic. I've known two worlds: that of today in which, near and next to everyone, everyone communicates with everything and everyone, and the other, the preceding one, in which a meticulous cutting up of islets would toss our detached lives about amid a space of scattered tatters. I quite like my granddaughter's recent remark: why did that stupid Robinson forget his mobile phone?

Were our fathers, in the middle of the river rumbling with fury, further separated from their wives than in ordinary times and on land? Georges, the dredger's wife was an alcoholic and would fall into fits of delirium tremens; cold and hard, the boss's wife didn't engage in tenderness. Might as well work. Might as well sail. Might as well fight against the current. Might as well spend your days and nights in the cold and risks. Might as well brave the elements. At least, adventure. Without love, work, the danger of death. Simultaneously, the dredger's wife drank because the man would work without taking any interest in her, and the other had hardened for the same reason, alone the two of them, without knowing whether their husbands would return or perish drowned amid the April waters. Former times, force of the world, separation of things, solitude of the sexes. But no distance separated the boss from the dredger, the fight on the barge having long since erased class warfare. In solidarity, they appreciated one another; they wouldn't have been able to live without each other; faced with risk, they formed a silent couple where each knew what the other was doing; they loved each other through Garonne, their common mistress. And the bitch, passionately loved, was not easy to deal with, either.

I was a child of sound enough health, but with a soul that was undermined by this same lack of love. This frail being had to face those wars that transformed part of the population, quiet and sane when living in peace, into a neurotic band of implacable policemen, denunciatory ideologues, sicarians, torturers, against a fringe group of heroes. How does this metamorphosis happen? I don't know, but I've seen it happen in certain circumstances. Sometimes, even today, I have the feeling that this or that person around me, patient and gentle, sometimes learned, could suddenly transform into an indiscriminate murderer should events and dogma shift. And the group frightens me; violent, always ready to become ferocious. Persons sometimes kill; the collective always kills.

From 1936 to 1956, four or five wars, tens of millions dead. I therefore did the same thing as Georges and the boss: devoted myself to things, river or sea. But the same metamorphoses have to be faced there. Neither good weather nor the summer lasts; floods come, along with storms, cyclones, masses of water in motion, the cataracts that turn the boat into a ping-pong ball struck at random by a hammer. It wants your hide, like the traitor of just now, but without any underhanded intention or hatred. If you get out of it, you're reborn from the ordeal without any resentment or spirit of vengeance. On the contrary: with the peaceful pride of having drunk the wine of the strong. I have therefore withstood, adult, proud, yes, full of pride, yes, Sea Ten and younger, those ferocious floods.

Dreamed enough, for, suddenly, the *traversier* is vibrating with something other than *bagassé*. A message of horror. Entangled in the cable and the branches, a corpse, a man in sandals, which we see from behind, his black hair scattering in the current, with streaks of blood, torn shirt, arms extended. Who is it?

This had already happened to us, while dredging one peaceful summer morning in low waters; the bucket chain had torn the cut from the repugnant remains of a murder so old that the police, once called, never discovered the identity of the victim; the murderer must have lived, for a long time, covered by the statute of limitations. But I could see that this dead man didn't drown either; the current turned him over; he had wounds on his face like hammer blows; a gaping cut opened his belly, like that of a pig emptied of its entrails. I still have in my memory today this apparition of crime, of the victim, of death in person, like the human image in miniature of the infernal commotion amid which we had been thrown. In the blind wall of nonsense, this corpse pierces a window through which a truth passes. What to do with the body? We didn't need this extra load, but we couldn't let it go drifting off. We made it slide off the cable into the *sapinou* and hauled ourselves toward the dredger. After having hoisted it onto the deck, we wrapped it in the greasy rags that were lying around the motor and left it in the hold until the flood stopped. Amid the permanent dangers and in the middle of the wild waters, we had perhaps even subsequently forgotten about it a little. No, I sometimes went down from the deck into the hold in order to see, in the darkness, this torn body. I was reflecting: since it was still floating underwater, it had, perhaps, been thrown upstream so that we would discover it at the obstruction of our cables and so that, with everyone blocked by the water, no one would be able to inform the police for a long time. During the recovery, Georges and the boss had exchanged a quick look, strange, filled with emotion, ill at ease, informed in some way. Did they know him? Did they not want to say anything about it? I kept quiet. But I swore to know more.

I'm stopping here, reader, at the risk of disappointing you. I was going to, as you guessed, tell a detective story. Now no longer, not here. We see ten of them a day on television, and even more in the store windows of the bookstores. Every time, ad nauseam, the interest of the mystery to be solved strings together a villainous crime, a gun or a dagger, red blood and a murderer, crime and punishment, base passions, terror and pity. Archaic, ineradicable, monstrous, unconscious, human sacrifice returns every day among us. Not here; never again that. We claim to have eradicated guilt, of religious origin, the learned say. How does it happen that secular and atheist societies, drugged by spectacle, continually invite us to search for he who has killed? To find the guilty party. We're bathed more by narratives whose interest comes from spilt blood than by floodwaters.

I'm cutting my narrative, suspenseful you suppose, far from gorging myself on corpses and convictions. Leave the police in peace, and let our sleeping base passions lie.

First Decision of Justice

Nevertheless, and since we are in hell, at least in that of water and blood, the question of evil returns. Too abstract, thus named, how do we recognize evil in everyday life? By the violence. Evil causes harm and puts to death. Howls, strikes, wounds, rapes, kills. That's the corpse hanging on my cable. The question of evil is then translated into the other, effectively omnipresent in all our spectacles: who has done violence? I cannot avoid it.

We establish tribunals to judge offenses and crimes; we seek to say who the culprit is. Who? A question in the singular. It's precisely that one that I'm abandoning for another, rarer, that we never pose, in the plural. In other words, do murderous societies exist? Yes, we answer, and – no doubt so as not to look at ourselves – we cite the Nazis, the Stalinist party, the sicarians of Pol Pot ... under the heading of crimes against humanity.

Have we now thought more deeply about the crimes of the collective, whichever it may be, even when it doesn't have some bloody madman at its head? Can we find a single society that, in the course of its history, has never declared war, never had its own children killed by its neighbors while killing its neighbor's children, never committed the crime of selling arms, persecuted some minority, hanged slaves and foreigners, stoned adulterous women, condemned innocents to death, sung of, glorified ten murderers praised in the history books and statufied on horseback in public squares? Which one, in addition, never waged war on the world by devastating rivers and seas? Murderers, all societies have lived in the state of mortal sin for millennia. Of original sin? Yes, original, since the blood of a scapegoat victim, lynched, glues the collective together, murderous so as to establish itself. How does it happen that society accuses and punishes an individual who, perchance, has killed, while no society, no individual accuses society which, for its part, always kills? For, killer, the collective collects itself by killing. What authority one day called together will accuse every group of murder? The abolition of the death penalty takes the first step in that direction. You, society, you no longer have the right to kill.

In such-and-such case, a jury judges the guilty party. Doubt for the individual. Who, on the other hand, with a global enough view and intelligence, will decide the culpability of God, if he exists, for having created floods and inundations, diseases or earthquakes? An undecidable decision for a creator, absent at least. But –

oh, certitude – do we know a single collective without the stain of blood? Let's convene a tribunal where the accusation of evil would no longer reside solely with an ordinary individual, nor God himself, with his undecidable existence, but in turn with all the societies of history and the world, all of them quite real. Which one, innocent of murders, would have its case dismissed for lack of evidence?

Egodicy: sometimes guilty, often innocent. *Theodicy*: undecidable sentence. *Sociodicy*: always guilty. Political thanatocracy, human and collective thanatomania.

Off the River's Mouth

Where did this corpse come from? Who was it? Who killed it? I don't know. I won't try to find out. I refuse to get vengeance for it. And I only see Garonne. For our victims, today, are the rivers, too. Their waters have irrigated my life, enchanted my thought, invigorated my body; I've known them to be threatening, untamable, as dangerous as the sea when it rages. Yes, murderous.

They decided to control their courses; dams, sometimes senseless, destroying sites and valleys, reduced entire populations to servile displacements; programs for the irrigation of thirsty farmland, often beneficial of course, completed their drying up. Exhausted by cotton, the Amu Darya, the Syr Darya no longer feed the Aral Sea, which is languishing and going to die; the Colorado and a good many others in the West, no longer flow into the sea; bled dry, even lives as well as my own, has recently become so weak that it no longer pushes its final sands out into sea, so that near its mouth, a new island has emerged, low and flat, as though born from it.

The lost body, there it is. Reborn, it lies not far from Cordouan, surfaced as a sand bank over several hectares above the water, pecked at by the seagulls as they happen to fly and defecate by, strewn with seaweed. Biogean, Earth and life. Gone downstream from Agen to the open of the ocean, "here lies" the one forgotten from the flood. I will never know who killed that man; may their soul be saved. That death symbolizes the murder of the rivers. Who then killed Garonne's strength? She is crowned by a birth. Metamorphosed into a lagoon, I recognize this newborn, this reborn being with its sandy complexion, in the middle of the open vagina of the Gironde losing her waters, weakened by her labor, amid the vortex of the tides.

Like Georges or the boss, what philosopher thinks like a river? Better, who, today, not only sees like the sea, dying, or the rivers, weakened, but also thinks like the entire Biogea, the entirety of the Earth and the living species? Like the victim Biogea? Will this thought, one day, be able to pacify us?

Who worries about the death pangs of the rivers? Who has ever read, in the course of one's studies, or heard those honored by history echoed by what river currents say? Yet we will, tomorrow, be dramatically thirsty. What thought, what politics are worth anything if they don't plan on watering the children, at risk of dying unquenched?

Hymn in Mesopotamia

In my body flows Garonne. I leave the train station of the town of my birth dry-eyed, but let me pass the Pont de Pierre and I will cry. My tears, licked, taste of the same water, below me, a me fluidified by it when I make headway on it. Let me injure myself and the Tarn opens, red, onto my bleeding skin. Aneto laments and sobs Garonne, which pours her tears mixed with mine out into the ocean, at Cordouan. But I sometimes think she's crying with joy, like me. In my organism, the fluids, upstream, come from Garonne in order to go downstream to her. My life slides in this flowing slipknot or corkscrews in this eddy.

From the bridge, on her, at Beauregard, seen from a distance, I perceive the fluvial series from above as a liquid vulva, in its long-limbed bed, with raised labia-shores of poplars. Never stop making love to Garonne. And being born from her, emerging, streaming, from my mother house with its watercress floor, its gravel

24

borders, its walls of reeds and willows, its ceiling of clouds under a pastel sky, a flowing house, wedding room, conjugal bed, beloved woman, birth canal, childhood swims during my fish age, heroic labors during the hard springs of the floods, womb from which I was driven away when I became a solitary wanderer of the Earth. But my flesh keeps her mother waters.

Descending twice from the middle of Garonne: from the line between the banks where the current flames and where the family boat dredged, but also from the center of the great descent between the *Trou du Toro* and Bordeaux, my bargeman's lineage held in its hands as a third party the upstream mountains and the downstream sea. I have received as an inheritance two Mesopotamian Edens.

Even the Seine, so well-behaved, even the Saint Lawrence, beautiful, or the Nile, so archaic, Yangtze or Amazon, everything that rolls outside my body still flows there like Garonne. Without ever being able to decide whether they came from her or from me, from the Niagara or the Yellow Sea, I found my Garonne blood and tears again in the seas and rivers of the world. The age-old union of her bed and floods with my veins and arteries reproduced my entire life before lakes and torrents. I gushed forth from her water, from the same water the world was born.

We are always swimming in this same river. Its peaks and shores crumble; the rocks erode, the humus mixes with the alluvial torrent, but not a single liquid molecule has gone missing in Garonne since the beginning of the world. Hard, the solid doesn't last; only soft water lasts. Under the sun, from April to October, this fluid evaporates, running everywhere in wandering clouds, but with the rumbling thunderstorm, here are the same snows, the same rains and the same waves, returned. We are always swimming in this same water that – statistically – turns, whose round clock indicates less the temporal than the eternal. Nothing could be more stable in memory and history than the processual turbulence that eddies in this vortex, like in my body – that middle-knot of Garonne – and like that divine wind that, they say, blew upon the primal waters, in a cyclone. In my body and across the world, Garonne circulates. My time goes and life passes, this eddy remains.

Having become a philosopher today, I think like the dying sea or a river in its death throes, like the divine sea or the paradise river, soft wombs of rebirth.

Earth and Mountains

You recognize a good pianist by his touch: delicate, powerful, velvety, living. A talented skier thus caresses the snow and a virtuoso of alpinism does the wall: skin, my powder snow; rock, my lover. A writer has a super-sharp sense for words; you read him sensitive to the rhythm, to the internal music of his language, to the sonorities of his syntactical structure, to the voice of the vowels. A scientist immediately senses the newness of a thorny detail. A philosopher, thus, has all his senses open.

Bang! 7.2 on the Richter scale. An enormous monster beneath my feet is shaking its back to rid itself of the little insects bothering it: us. Everything is collapsing; the walls shudder; men and women fall. For tens of long seconds, like an organ deep beneath the ground, thunder rumbles with anguish and high beauty. In fact, an earthquake lasts weeks; over the following days, reminding aftershocks took place, sometimes less: five, four and a half … on the same scale, sometimes more powerful than the first blow, unpredictably.

Then, the body discovers a completely different relation to the Earth. If it shakes again, the body will know how to measure the intensity of the superficial shuddering. Three, I sleep, the body unaltered. No, four's not serious. Six and up, I run and protect myself. I remember having felt these symphonic bones and this awake epidermis being born after the Loma Prieta earthquake of 1989, along the San Andreas Fault, where I finally became a being-in-the-world, the way formerly, on the rolling floor of my bridge, the Ocean made me into a being-at-sea. At that time, my body transformed into a sensitive seismograph that had no need of any machine to estimate precisely how and how much the Earth was shaking. Eminently adapted, my sensation caresses and follows the fissure's trembling.

Since then, my body thinks like the Earth. In his *Sand County Almanac*, which is worth quite a few philosophical treatises, our good Aldo Leopold already said: *thinking like a mountain*. Erotic, this finely diversified, velvety receptivity to the snow, the rock face, the sea, the earth … resembles the talent of the caress. Among the stiff and cold skins, there are delicious partners and silky lovers.

Earth, my hard and soft mistress.

HARD EARTH. SECOND DECISION OF JUSTICE

The substratum speaks, thunders and kills. It resounds and vibrates like the Deluge and the river flood, which, in their turn, howl like wolves. It will be necessary for me to hear the voices of the living. But, in the meantime, who was guilty, back then, of these thousand victims? After the tsunami of Lisbon, in the XVIIIth century, Voltaire and the Enlightenment reached a verdict and accused God whose creative act permitted these horrors. That decision seems undecidable, at least in absentia.

Yet the balance of judgment is quickly decided, here: at 7.2, the Loma Prieta quake which I suffered from but which delighted me, caused some material damage and fifty-seven victims, whereas two hundred and fifty thousand Haitians died in Port-au-Prince, recently, for less intensity on the Richter scale. Human, collective, political, economic, social conditions – poverty for example – prevail, and by far, over the purely physical cause. Voltaire and the Enlightenment were mistaken: only society can be accused.

Where I find the first sentence again.

And my interfering epidermis, so sensitive to the slightest shaking of the ground. This receptivity is comprehensible. For like the atoms of things, the *ego* radiates with valences. An octopus, equipped with eight tentacles, a starfish, Briareus or Vishnu with a hundred arms, a neuron adapted to a hundred synapses ... everything happens as though the *ego* – echo of a thousand voices – throughout its life was sweeping across the periodic classification of the elements, taking on in passing more and more numerous connections. Carbon and oxygen me, gold, silver and metal me, even rare earth. The value of someone, that is to say his health, is measured by the number and the quality of his valences. Through these pseudopod bunches, at the extremities of which delicate sensibility takes place, he picks up, receives and welcomes others, sometimes thusly equipped. Through these emanating channels, he sometimes becomes others, becomes his male or female neighbor. He caresses her, he offers to penetrate her, she refuses or accepts. I think, therefore I flow into an other.

I think like the wounded man on the road, especially as, Samaritan, I'm passing here through a country that considers me to be a public enemy, the excluded and hated other. Here I am other facing an other whose two egos come together. Not taking himself for a subject, the first doesn't turn the other into an object, thrown, at a distance, before: sympathetic, he knows his suffering, transports him, anoints him, bandages him, pays for his care, gives him life again; and becomes his fellow man, his neighbor in the superlative, with no more distance, skin to skin in some way, at the least pitying look at the imploring face. The two valences go in concert.

When I caress my girlfriend, my eyes magnify her gaze, my sense of touch clothes and exalts her skin that glorifies mine. The *ego* lives and has value from creating *ego* in others who can, then, pay it back tenfold, in life and value. Without this creativity of others, toward them and through them, with them and in them – valences radiate along the paths opened up by prepositions – the *ego*, sickly, autistic, sick, castrated of its valences, without value, devoid of health … annihilates, breaks, destroys the *ego* of others. Like the torpedo fish, to which the narcissus owes its name, the egoist strikes the neighbor down with narcotic torpor. The only things that exist around him are objects, well-named since he projects or rejects them. Then, hell is other people. Contrary to this pathetic destruction, I think, therefore I become he or she about whom I am thinking.

Now here today are other neighbors, constituents of the Biogea: the sea, my lover; our mother, the Earth, become our daughter; this beautiful breeze which inspires the spirit, a spiritual mistress; our light friends, the fresh and flowing waters; and our brothers, the living things ... are henceforth no longer objects. Scholars or not, we presuppose, almost unbeknownst to us, that puritanical distinction between the subject, me or we, and said objects. We suffer from an *ego* armored with walls, with turtle shells, incapable of caressing. I prefer the Good Samaritan to this autism with its saurian or serpentine epidermis, the Good Samaritan with his velvety touch, whose access to the wounded man, lying in the ditch, testifies to a simply human sensitivity to the neighbor; his open behavior indicates a talented lover's skin. Subjects, we pave the world, I mean hell, with objects, named thus by us because thrown before us, rejected, better, disposable: trashcan-Earth, polluted air, dead seas, factory farmed fowl, feet welded into the cement, an unclean world, sewage fields, soiled by us for us to appropriate them. Destroyed by a collective that's narcissistic in its turn.

That the subject, collective or personal, determines objects in this way defines the reason of an admirable, useful science, to which we owe comfort and lucidity, but henceforth outdated; formerly admirable, its rational triumph hesitates today before unreasonable limits. This exact and precise process of objectivizing things lasted three centuries and amounts to one aspect, one face, a partial work of reason, which today has more and better to do before the certain agony of things and men, an agony due, precisely, to this objectivization, due, in turn, to the definition of a subject deprived of valences. Decision and exclusive division: on one side, this subject, personal or collective, royal; on the other, the passive and submissive objects, reduced to a few dimensions of space, time, mass, energy and power, almost naked, undressed, bloodless. Simplistic and naive, implacable, of an unparalleled cruelty, this way of knowing accompanied fields of knowledge that today we find easy: the sciences said to be hard, objective, whose royal supremacy, until recently uncontestable, is drawing to an end. We are changing paradigm.

In a different way more difficult, subtle and complete, the life and Earth sciences, henceforth put in the center of cognition, take over. They practice a more sharing, open, connected way of knowing, in which he who knows participates in the things he knows, is even reborn from them, tries to speak their language, listens to their voices, respects their habitat, lives the same evolutionary history, is enchanted by their narratives, limits finally, through them or for them, his power and his politics, so oddly named after the city, from which the Biogea is absent. The life and Earth sciences are once again sewing together the tear that was separating the subject and its objects. Dare I say that they become human from it? Yes, I am what I think which is also me; I am who I caress and what I feel. Unburdened of its exclusive prerogatives and having decided to give up a part of them, the knowing subject objectivizes itself, the object cognitivizes itself.

Stripped by highwaymen – my ancestors and contemporaries – you are begging for mercy below the ditch that runs alongside my route; I hear you, subject Biogea, thrown below, oh, my neighbor. I weigh on her who weighs on me, I think like her.

Gaping Earth

To think like her, I first listen to her voice, the way I heard the floods and the substratum. Beneath rumbling Etna's chimneys, our Ancients believed that Vulcan, a blacksmith, was striking the anvil with a sledgehammer; that Jupiter, from Mt. Olympus, was hurling thunder and lightning, bursting in the ears; that Neptune and the Nereids were undulating in the roaring tides while the skirts of the Hamadryads were luffing in the crown of the trees and Aphrodite was inciting the reciprocal prayer by which the sexes call upon one another. In a word, they put the gods in charge of proclaiming the Biogea.

Yet, no religious festival from Ancient Rome seems more evocative to me than the one during which, three times a year, on August 24th, October 5th and November 8th of our calendar, on Mont Palatine, not far from the cave where the She-Wolf found, new-born, the twins and suckled them, the Biogea – ordinarily closed, and without the aid of any god or any signal on their part – opened its mouth to let the unworldly lament of the dead through. The feast was called: *Mundus patet*; the world opens; the Earth yawns or gapes wide.

In Iceland, the Andes or California, not to mention the open maws of volcanoes, Mount Etna or Hawaii, you can see furrows just about everywhere in the world gape in this way over seismic and hot faults that are similar to the one that was supposed to have opened then in the Roman Forum. The Biogea's vaginas? Seated in the midst of the vapors emanating from a similar thermal opening, the pythia of Delphi deliriously uttered words thought to precede meaning by her contemporaries.

Yet I think that our Roman ancestors were mistaken about the meaning and the sounds emanating from the tectonic gaping. Since they didn't understand the commotion emanating from the dark bowels of the ground, they interpreted the yawning that came out of the fault as the words of phantoms coming back from the depths of the Underworld. They acted like we, citizens, do; they humanized, they politicized the world. No, the dead don't speak or sing or weep or howl; their dust and bones remain silent forever. This commotion, this noise, this rumbling emanating out of the cavern and its dark masses comes from the world itself, without any superfluous masks, dead or gods. *Mundus patet*: a strange noise emanates from the ground, torn open on that day. Can I decipher its meaning?

Meaning? We don't hear anything but it; we don't know anything but it. We give it the names Vulcan, Jupiter, the spirits of the ancestors … meaningful proper names of meaningful human gods or meaningful corpses that only know meaning, the meaning suitable for covering over the rumble of things, meaningless. Now, precisely evident, open, blaring – we don't hear anything but it – meaning always emanates from some material channel or medium, a vocal cord, a column of air or a metal plate; invisible, astride the sound waves and issuing from these signals, it flies over them. Now, when it passes away, the very material of the channel remains, the physical consistency of the metal and its heat, the innermost vibration of the atoms that go to make up the cord or vibrate along the organ column. The clamor of things or the background noise of the world.

The Romans had a genius, which we have lost, for partially opening from time to time the shadow mouth of those things that whisper, but they had already lost them as well, and for some time, the genius for directly perceiving the untranslatable mystery of those noises whose voices only Orpheus, long ago, had attempted to reproduce on his lyre. And, panicked, they covered these infernal rumblings with divine figures, speaking and meaningful. Meaning protects us from fear.

Good citizens, the Romans loved history, as we do, and commemorated their dead. Did they hear the rumbling emanating from that hole better than we do? I praise those who invented this festival. Not through any obligation to remember or to be reminded to avenge the dead, but for another reason, nobler and more profound. Who among us, since that time, has ever celebrated the opening of such a shadow door? An audacity of genius was needed to call forth those dark masses. At least the Romans loosened that seismic fault, that caldera, that cavern, that pit, that chimney. Where is this mouth to be found in our deaf modern times? Closed, every door that opens onto the world. Where is the passage to be found?

SECOND MEDITATION ON OUR WAYS OF KNOWING
To amaze the crowd and get himself talked about, an artist wrapped bridges, buildings, statues in public squares. I see, I hear, I know the world wrapped with words, sentences, images. We put birds in cages, fish in aquariums, plants in pots, children in schools, adults in factories and offices, women under veils or in houses, God under the low crushing masses

of stone in the churches of the countryside and the naves of the cathedrals, our love letters in envelopes, lastly, for settlement in full, all the things of the world in prison under words, locked up behind their bars. This so-called artist gives expression to this general wrapping.

I would like to listen to the things freed of these packages, the way they presented themselves before finding themselves named. Betelgeuse disappeared into the bag of its star naming; I only eat asparagus or carrots folded in bunches in the daily newspaper of their appellation; I see winds and rains below their satellite image map; your first name and your words hide your body from me and even, almost, your voice, your voice which, in its turn, names me. For thousands of years, we have been licking things with our tongues, covering and daubing them so as to appropriate things for ourselves. If language boils down to a convention, this convention took place between the speakers without consulting the thing named, become as a result the property of those who covered it in this way with their drawn or voiced productions. *Malfeasance* analyzes these acts of appropriation.

Thus every inert object, every living thing as well, sleeps under the covers of signs, a little in the way that, today, a thousand posters shouting messages and ugly riots of color drown, with their filthy flood, the landscapes, or better, exclude them from perception because the meaning, almost nil, of this false language and these base images forms an irresistible source of attraction to our neurons and eyes. This appropriation covers the world's beauty with ugliness. How to estimate at their exact thickness the layers of media under which all things lie, thus multiply wrapped under writings, folded under printed matter, gagged under images, hidden under sounds, choked under languages, lost under a hundred screens? A screen, quite a confession: obstructing as much as revealing.

One intelligent instructor once told me that certain of his pupils, among the most gifted, seemed to be grieving from having suddenly entered into writing. Did they remember a world without words, before any learning of saying and reading? Were they weeping over a second loss? Of what use to us were certain neurons of the left occipito-temporal region of our brain before we re-employed them recently – less than three thousand years – for reading? The most expert specialists in cognitive science pose this question as well.

Burying things in a first glove of words, a second pocket of writing, a third screen of printed matter, a thousand names. Black boxes, reliquaries, prisons, our safes belonging to the fabulously wealthy owners of everything in the world, without exception. The way our right-handers help themselves to the straight line, orientation or the law, our language conventions cover things so as to appropriate them.

Freed from these pockets, these chests, I would like to see them reborn under their code proper name. And myself, aren't I called Michel Serres by pure and simple convention? The coding of my DNA says my true proper name. For liberating the things, emancipating them, making us be reborn with them in this way, this is knowing them.

GAPING MOUTH

At least the Romans took two or three days in order to rip up these fabrics, put holes in these pockets and hiding places, to break the padlocks, spread the lips of these faults and look the unworldly pit in the face, to hear the things as such, rid of these packages. They unglued these envelopes to better read the things, not to the letter, but unlettered! Forebears as ancient as their oblivion had invented gods in human form in order to cover, once again, the things with bodies, flesh, images and voices, meanings, the way we cover them with names or posters, with ideas, that is to say, with idols. Since they were afraid of the sea, they decked it out with an icon armed with a trident followed by a thousand young women whose fish tails veiled the waves with their charm; since they were distressed over the day and its light, they veiled it with the gentle name of Father; since lightning terrified them, they softened it with a Jupiter hurling spears. They hid the world by means of persons who resembled them, the way we hide it beneath screens where directors play the role of false gods.

No, these gods don't say the sea or the trees, but are silent about them, if I dare say, hide them, plug them up, seal them off, distort them, prevent them from emitting; consequently, prevent us from hearing their rumbling; the gods transform their noise into pseudo-divine words, human in fact. Narcissistic, humans metamorphose the things of the world into women and men. We subjugate them; we politicize them beneath words and the best among us put them into equations. A little shadow of lie beneath the brilliance of truth.

The ancient Romans had the intelligence and daring to sweep aside that puppet population in cardboard décor for three days, to look these things, this world in the face through a black opening, and, through this gaping hole, listen directly to a frightful clamor. I admire their audacity in this and respect this festival. I confess it, I don't know what is said there; but I wouldn't want to die before understanding anything about it. Bring your ear near this abyss.

Mundus latet. The world is hidden. We hide the Biogea. Who sees it, yes, who hears it? *Mundus patet*: in those days, it opened, manifest, revealed itself, said itself, but we, Latins, no longer understand anything about the noise of the lead shot, latent, that emanates from this hole, about this tumult preparative to an earthquake, from which, patiently, the dazzling meaning of our languages emerged billions of years later. *Mundus patet*: I've decided that the dates August 24th, October 5th and November 8th shall become national holidays in Biogea. We'll celebrate then the infernal hole, the source, the gaping mouth of every narrative in this book, the bottom of a horn of plenty that I'm trying to open today. For I'm searching for the meaning of this fundamental hubbub, in its nascent state. The Biogea rustles; it shouts on the nether side of our languages; without them; below them; outside them; beneath these lines, before the meaning of what I am saying gushes forth.

Bergschrund

Yes, I've often seen the opened Earth, and I've even heard cries come out of its gaping opening, like the ancient Romans. Better, between the lips of that opening, I've been present at births. Like this.

Any alpinist has crossed crevasses. Gray, black, sometimes mauve, always blue-green, wide or narrow, they threaten and yawn: gaping Earth. On a snow bridge or otherwise, no one crosses them without fear and trembling, particularly bergschrunds, those indentations, sometimes a thousand meters deep, at the vertical of rock faces and at the birth of glaciers, as though born from their contact. I'm pleased to have crossed, in dreading them, those crevassed rivers of ice before they die; I've seen them, little by little, grow shorter and sometimes disappear. You can fall into the hell of their gaping openings, you can also come out of them. Like this.

We were descending – Anne-Marie, brave and beautiful, Jean-Yves, our saintly guide, and me – from the Barre des Écrins, and with the morning over we were getting ready to cross the final bergschrund before a break at the hut past the glacial crossing. The leader of the roped party took the usual measures, a solid anchor and two or three lengths of rope. Anne-Marie went forward and, as never happens, the snow bridge gave way and she disappeared without a cry into the abyss. After having checked the anchor again, Jean-Yves and I, our hearts beating wildly, crawled to the upper lip of the crevasse and called: "Anne, Anne-Marie!" From below, a voice answered us, unrecognizable, whose tonality surprised us; but anxiety can deform the throat and ice walls echo. Even stranger: that call seemed to ask for a rope, while, duly tied and strapped in, our friend had no need for any additional link. Jean-Yves sent one all the same, and as soon as we were assured with a shout that she could climb back up, we hauled her up with all our might. Fatigue, obstacles, ice ridges, getting stuck to the limits of breaking, prudence, the ascent lasted a long time, in the anxiety that it might fail.

But finally we thought we were going to faint in seeing emerge from the edges of the crevasse … a man. We were expecting a black-haired woman; a blond male emerged in her stead. A terrifying apparition. I can still see this pale, groaning, unexpected phantom come out of the ground, like the open lips of a caesarian.

We were soon to learn that we had just rescued another alpinist who, doing the same route solo, had fallen into the bergschrund two days previously and was slowly dying from cold, hunger and abandonment. Resigned, he had even stopped shouting when, changed into an ice statue after two nights of agony, he heard calling not far from him. His desperate voice covered over the cries of our friend.

Of course, quickly, quickly, we extirpated, as well, our Anne, angel, from the white-black and cold hell. With humor and bravura, she shook herself: "That was a narrow escape, wasn't it?" she laughed, deep-frozen. With leaping hearts, we couldn't stop hugging her. Not only to warm her up. After the first treatments for the escapees – survival blankets and hot tea from the flask – after the final descent, slow, all four fed, reassured, relaxed around Kronenbourgs at the hut, we calculated the rare chance that the snow bridge should have given way beneath the one at the very same spot where the other had been victim, before, of a similar accident. What luck this misfortune. Drunk with joy, more saintly than ever, Jean-Yves, standing on the table, sang: "I found my Eurydice … with a second Orpheus … I have the right to drink even more than Noah."

For that morning the Earth gaped and twice gave birth.

Gaping Mother-Earth

These newborn adults, where do they live, in what house, at what address? In the cavity of the bergschrund, two nights; on board the Ark on the Black Sea, four times ten days; on Garonne, during the floods, on the fragile pontoon boat that dredges up the river's memory … next everywhere in the Biogea's immensity. Where does it lie, for its part? Here, there? In a word, what is a place?

A genital word, quite precisely. However far back I go into the origins or roots of my language, "place" [*lieu*] designates, as with the shores of the river or the lips of the crevasse by which the world opens, "place" traces, I was saying, in our mother tongues, Greek and Latin, the vulva, the vagina, the female genitalia – gaping mother – the uterus or the womb, the embryo's habitat for nine months, as well as the canal by which every newborn passed and will pass. Here are our escapees again!

The womb body. Because he was, that day, expelled from the belly of his mother – a supremely blessed locale, more comfortable than the white and black crevasse from which Anne-Marie as well as the blond phantom were born, more inhabitable than the Deluge from which humanity was reborn – every human finds himself, outside, delocalized. Where did he live formerly? Here, in the womb, in the warmth, nourished, lodged, curled up, cradled. But where now? Wandering in space, exposed to the high seas, he dreams, more or less, of returning to the lost paradise. The sexual and reproductive system of women, this place, the bottom of the torso, becomes the Eden of origins, high with dream. Hard with blood and narrow passage, soft with strange nostalgia.

The local soil. Thus named, is the human born from humus or from flesh? Those are two variations on the womb of origin and of habitat. The place passes then from life to the Earth through their open proximity. Gaping Mother-Earth: whether of body or of silt, a gaping opening yawns in the middle of the Biogea, at the weld between Bio and Gea, from which our origin and my book springs up.

The law. Now, before every birth, the laws often hesitate between *jus sanguinis* and *jus soli*, as though they poorly distinguished this cavity, this caesura, where the earth and flesh diverge. Conversely, might law itself be born, like us, from this place of rootedness where life and soil join, from this middle between Bio and Gea, as though it was beginning to settle human children on the Earth?

The bloody history. Political power seeks then to defend, in the event of attack, this soil, that of a fatherland – without the vile appropriation by the males we ought to say *motherland* – which then asks its children to give their lives and spill their blood to protect it. So, this land is theirs because, soiled by blood and appropriated by it, the land covers the bodies of those who died for it, who bled on it, like a parturient. We are, at the price of these carnages, once again localized. But this putative fatherland cannot demand such sacrifices of its sons without appealing, even if it doesn't acknowledge it, to the sacred. A passage from low tombs to a few sublime evocations; hard cemeteries under pseudo-soft hymns, like the bloody *Marseillaise*.

Pagan religion. Thus sacralized by these sacrifices, the place becomes holy land. Derived from the Latin *pagus*, which designates the plot of land worked by the peasant and beneath which his ancestors sleep in peace, paganism settles its pagans onto their land. They are, at the price of this effort and death, once again localized. So powerfully that wandering and emigration are experienced as tortures. From Ovid to Du Bellay, how many poets have lamented exile, homesickness, both the *saudade* and the *Heimweh*.

A sudden thunderclap. The holy land is no longer there, but lies elsewhere, far off, in Palestine, in the places where Abraham stopped, where Jesus Christ was born, suffered, died and was risen. Perhaps it isn't seen well enough just what an enormous anthropological revolution the conversion of the paganisms to Christianity triggered: the land on which we lived, the soil that we worked and defended lost the sacred and became profane, secularized. From then on, we were born from elsewhere. In its turn, the entire country found itself, like every one of us, delocalized. Indifferent, therefore, objectivizable. An objective science and technological intervention in life and the Earth then became possible and permissible. Separate, independent, from then on subjects, we faced objects, thrown there. All of us, children of Eve, are exiles.

Except, no doubt, those who still inhabit the holy land or holy lands, where blood is flowing and will always flow, no doubt, alas, for the same, archaic, tragic and absurd reason.

A modern religion. One more step and this conversion became generalized: the holy land was not to be found anywhere in concrete space. City of God, Heavenly Jerusalem, the true city rises in another world. The entire Earth deterritorialized. A total transfer from the low, strangely desacralized by the religious, high. Delocalized too, humanity lives then, here or there in fact, but elsewhere for heads, symbols and ideals. As a result, it temporarily became a renter. And the renter enjoys a double place: for he lives in the place he inhabits, but he is all the same not from there since he is not the owner.

The temporary rented location. We are from here, from life and the Earth, but we aren't from here. Always individual, sometimes collective, death makes this double location easy to think. We will all depart and leave the Earth to others than us, whose habitat will continually pass to others and to others, indefinitely. We live in a rented location; not only on the Earth, in Gea, but also in Bio, I mean in our bodies, which carry within them what, indefinitely, makes the opening for the relay of the species. The body is not only for itself, it carries in itself for those that follow, as well. I live my body in transitive rented location.

The new habitation. For if we, renters, have to assume the responsibility of maintaining a merely temporary habitat, quite common to everyone across space and time, in order to pass it on to successors as habitable and beautiful as we received it from our predecessors, without soiling it with blood or other stains so as to appropriate it for ourselves, we must live, in some way, at the same time there and outside the there, between here and elsewhere, in the opening between two worlds, in the place of our loves and our works, certainly, but at the same time apart, in the symbolic and the concrete, the second receiving its meaning from the first. Failing this temporary rented location, thus open and gapped, a third death would arise on our horizon: the eradication of our species, the disappearance of the human race. That is a limit-hell whose current pregnance induces us to frequent an elsewhere. No doubt we have our feet on the Earth, hard, and our heads in the soft.

Our contemporary knowledge. That is, how and where to live; that is the status of the Biogea. The history of language, religion, of secular law and politics here agrees, in a way that's urgent for our survival, with our most recent knowledge. For from now on in the center of our thoughts, the life and Earth sciences designate, between these two kingdoms, the same open place – gaping Biogea – from which the social and human sciences will have to be reborn. Human: one hundred percent nature, one hundred percent culture. The Biogea produces such an overlapping.

The new opening. As low beneath our feet as you like, the Biogea opens us to another space, high enough for us to be able to acquire a wisdom there, that of redeveloping this same place differently from our fathers, this place that's still politically cut up by old hatreds, beneath the flood of tears and blood that we call history. Without this soft place, spiritually very old, but newly conceived in this way, without the juridical construction of a common good, opposed to our filthy ownership, I don't see how our planet, hard, will survive. Hardness that depends on a softness, material belonging that depends on this temporary rented location.

Low and hard, the hell of the Deluge, of the floods, of the crevasse; high and soft, the paradise of the sea, of Garonne and the mountains. For different reasons than in times past, we're traveling through similar places, sinister and sublime. We inhabit the Biogea, valley of labors and joys, but also frequent a place that we need in order to relativize our passions for possession, our stupidities of control, our cruel decision to objectivize the beings and things of the world, in short, our libido for belonging, and to detach ourselves from that will to appropriation that, already soiling the habitat of our children, is destroying their lives even before they are born.

But is the mind constantly soft?

Three Volcanoes

No. After these birthings from waters and earth, the four elements and their old order now lead me into the airs of joy and into the fires of knowledge, sometimes become the fires of hell.

FIRST FIRE: ETTORE MAJORANA

In the year preceding the explosion of the last world war, on the morning of March 25th, Annunciation Day, a young Italian boarded the regular mail-boat that connected the port of Naples to that of Palermo. His name appears on the passenger list; the police investigation established, according to eyewitnesses, that he took his place in his cabin.

Scarcely an adult, thirty-one years old, 1.70m, black hair, a deep scar on the back of one hand, this passenger had just made important discoveries in nuclear physics, on strong interactions. A calculator of the first order, admired by Fermi and Heisenberg, even arousing their jealousy, he came out of the great laboratories of Italy and Germany. Foreseeing in him the great scientist of the future, his peers had just appointed him full professor to the faculty of Naples, where he had assumed his post and taught for several months. In the middle of the academic year, no one knows why, he set sail for Sicily.

Born in Catania, at the foot of Mount Etna, on August 5, 1906, he disappeared on March 26, 1938. No trace of him was ever found.

If fascist Italy, Nazi Germany and the democratic countries, that is to say the future belligerent parties, were at that time expecting the explosion of world war, only a few extremely rare specialists were preparing or predicting that of atomic energy, stemming precisely from the forces of interaction. Ettore Majorana, for that is the young man's name, was one of them: "Physics has taken a bad path," he wrote.

Majorana boarded and disappeared. What became of him? To this day no one has solved the mystery. Suicide? Kidnapping? Murder? Bodies are always found. Only the living find a way to disappear, an old police adage asserts. With his own hand, ill-tempered, Mussolini himself wrote, in red ink, on the file concerning him: "I want him found."

The first solution, that of suicide, seems to be established by a letter to Carrelli, his director at the Naples Physics Institute. For before taking the steamship, Majorana wrote to him: "I've made an unavoidable decision. There is not the least trace of egoism in it … but I'm aware of the inconveniences my sudden disappearance could cause the students as well as you. I will keep a fond memory of all of you, at least until eleven o'clock this evening and, if possible, even after."

An enigmatic conclusion. A short letter intended for his family asked them, according to Sicilian custom, to mourn for three days and no more. There he was on the sea, pacing the gangways, pensive.

Better than talent, everyone recognized in him that global intuition that only belongs to the great names cited two or three times per century. When he obtained a considerable result, he opened up to his equals – Heisenberg or Fermi – about it, even giving it to them, and crumpled the papers on which he had recorded it before throwing them away. Thus, how many times did he allow his own ideas to be published by others?

Quiet, even withdrawn, he demonstrated an unparalleled modesty. One might have said that physics was debating itself in him without coming out, silent and as though vanished, it too, at the bottom of his chest. Those who work with books, tools, documents, as though knowledge opened, before them, in a place outside of them, differ from those who carry the adventure of science in their bodies and whose attention is focused in the light that inhabits them. These latter are in danger at the slightest circumstance.

Did he foresee the forces locked within the heart of the elements? Just as the Sicilians sometimes saw Mount Etna spew out its mauve lava or at least stain the horizon with glowing, did he see some fire rise from the forces of interaction? Did his silence conceal secrets that he wanted to keep, an originary fear stemming from the roots of knowledge? Which atomic volcano's voice did he listen to?

All the same Majorana did not die that day, nor that night. For as soon as he arrived in Palermo, he wrote a telegram to the same Carrelli: "The sea refused me. I'll return tomorrow to stay in the same hotel in Naples." Did he then re-embark from Sicily to Italy on the evening of March 26th, the exact date of the telegram? If yes, the young man must have disembarked the following day at the Italian port at 5:45. A final witness hesitates over the person with whom he shared his cabin that night. After these words, nothing more.

When he became one of the great figures of my youth, I believed he had been living for a long time, solitary, in his early sixties, a Trappist or Carthusian, retired, anonymous, in silence, in a cell of some monastery in Sicily or in the south of Italy. Did he foresee Hiroshima as he listened to Mount Etna? Is he lying today under some silent stone saying a saintly name in the garden behind the chancel of that enclosure?

Each of the hypotheses produced to explain his disappearance generates a different narrative: a spy novel, if a great power kidnapped the scientist; but we would know it since the fall of the Iron Curtain and the statute of limitations on the secrets of the Chancellery; a detective novel, if hidden interests had him murdered; a psychological narrative as well, for a recent trial, moving, implicated him and his family in a drama in which a small child died in its crib, burned alive, again by fire, but whose outcome exonerated his close relations. Or, without another word: he is dead; may his soul rest in peace.

Peace. We only learned seven years later, in August, 1945, what was being prepared in the laboratories during the years preceding the war. It's no longer a question, then, of a narrative, or a novel, or of the life of this person or that person, however much of a genius he might have been, but of the history of the world and of humanity, of one of the moments in which an alliance was formed between reason, said to be soft, and the most terrifyingly hard death. The original sin of nuclear physics, Hiroshima's flash marks this moment. Our history since then has been enveloped in that explosion, like a continuous wave. A child of Hiroshima, a son of Majorana, I live and think like a child of the war, an heir of the bomb.

How is it that the lights we receive from the sciences are sometimes accompanied by such blindnesses? The better we know, the more we can. How to go from these possibilities to the real without posing the problem of evil? What responsibility did the scientists of the Manhattan Project formerly bear?

May the soul of he who seemed to have had a premonition of the terrible conflict of science and the bomb rest in peace. A paper signed by one of his friends called him a prophet. Did he, in the jumble of equations, foresee the consequences, the chain of things or their unleashing? The experts are not all of the same opinion. Impossible, say the ones, to foresee the bomb in 1938. Others, it is also said, had announced it well before, since in 1921 a certain physicist declared: "We live on an island of gun cotton." That old explosive seems to us today to be as trifling as a child's toy.

Supposing that we had foreseen everything, what would we have done, us? One does not stop science, or progress, even less the necessity to win a just war, the libido of the dominant males that always drives them to show themselves to be the strongest of all, the fierce competition, the passion of small brains to arrive first, to win out over the others, and to be discovered before them. What difference is there between the scientific stars of the Manhattan Project, vainglorious and appearance-conscious like prima donnas, wanting to succeed at all costs, before the Nazi physicists, persuaded that the latter were on their way to making the bomb, and any one of us in today's laboratories, seeking to outstrip the others for some mediocre medal?

Does one stop the compulsion to defeat, including peaceful fights? Don't these latter make us forget the real stakes? In our culture, competition prevails over the order of the world. The neurosis of glory is the first served. Winning, arriving the first, becoming the strongest, obtaining the victory … finally, unleashing the maximal energy. One does not stop this progress, this progression, this climb, no, this descent into the Underworld. One fine day, this route to the summit became atomic escalation, the old and new thanatocracy, the power of and through death. It made a river of blood and tears flow (it perhaps also prevented one from flowing). One does not stop this volcano, its lava flow and rain of ash. One climbs the sides of the crater; falls into the chimney.

Born in Catania, vanished at Palermo, with a passion for naval fleets and battles, the young Majorana understood, descended the slope of that escalation, knew that at the end of the ascent, at the top of this progression, there is the gaping crater whose scorching voice the Sicilian peasants have always heard, a voice that the inhabitants of Hiroshima are going to have to suffer in their irradiated flesh.

He climbed back down. Calculated, solved, tore up the crumpled paper on which he wrote his problem, making his signature disappear. Did he seek to erase the traces of his body, of his name, of his work and discoveries? He taught, first, then stifled his voice. What else could he do to try to ward off the due date? He carried in himself a tragic moment of science; he erased the signs of it by smoothing out his sandal marks in the dust of the ground.

Still seeking old traces to reconstruct the events, *Voilà,* my old police investigation. Of no interest now; like that of the body caught on the cable during the flood. Far from reconstructing pre-war testimonies, I prefer to travel further, to a forgotten Antiquity in which to seek a meaning for this mystery.

An Island with Three Points

The Ancients sometimes called the island of Sicily: *Trinacria*, triangle, tricorne; three capes or promontories, three points stand out below the Italian boot. The Trapani point, to the west, at Erice, today hosts an Institute of physics that bears Majorana's name. In the hollow of the eastern point rises, up to three thousand meters, Mount Etna, a volcano threatening the surrounding populations with its lava.

On three continents and on its islands, the shores of the Mediterranean saw the birth of geometry, physics, chemistry, natural history, as well as philosophy and at least two, if not three monotheisms. The first paradise of the mind that I'm describing by itemizing the recent divisions, the specialties that were separated later, but mixed in the beginning. In the middle of these waters from which the West's reasons were born is an island seesawing between the eastern and the western sea, a land with three sides but also three scientists, so great they marked their times: Majorana, from Catania and Trapani; Archimedes, dead and born in Syracuse; lastly Empedocles of Agrigentum. That is, in two thousand five hundred years, a summary of our knowledge, our wisdom and our deadly lunacies. Paradise of the mind, volcanic hells.

Let us visit this island, take a tour around a microcosm, a mirror and symbol of the world, a tour of an ancient and contemporary history, a tour of science and its problems, a tour of what it's needful to know, do and believe, a tour of a formerly and recently unimaginable ethics. On every stage of the journey, at the end of every leg, a rumbling volcano awaits us. End of the first act, hell, the fire of Hiroshima.

Blaise Pascal called Archimedes the greatest in the order of the mind and compared him to Jesus Christ, first, for his part, in the order of charity. The modern period of the sciences began by collecting the scientist's legacy; we still think like his children. His inventions earn him every honor and glory.

A mathematician, he understood numbers like no one before him, he who had the audacity to take them in their immense growth, as though the grains of sand of the beach were invading the Universe. "Count them," he said, while putting a grain of this sand on the first square of a kind of chessboard, at the bottom, on the left, for instance, and two on the next square, then four on the one after that, and so on, doubling, each time, the stake. Quickly, the figure obtained, astronomical, surpassed the greatest fortune of the richest of kings. Likewise, the numerical solution to his famous cattle problem covers six hundred pages with figures. The account of the scientist from then on exceeded that of princes.

A geometer, he understood figures like no one before him, for he knew how to calculate, for instance, with precision, the ratio between the radius of a circle and its circumference, the number later called

62

π. In addition, he constructed magnificent curves, like the spiral or helix; in the depths of our cells, we carry our DNA like an Archimedean form. Lastly, he measured the parabola by using proportions and the lever, a machine allowing the weak and the small to withstand great forces and lift enormous weights. He intended, in this way, to shake the terrestrial globe itself: I would lift the Earth, he said, on condition of having a fulcrum. Thus, the strength of the scientist prevailed, by far, over all the world's powers.

An engineer, he understood equilibrium like no one before him, and in the subtlest and most difficult circumstances, in a liquid medium. By plunging the royal crown into water and assessing its volume and density, he knew how to decide the authenticity of the alloy or its falsity. Thus the scientist gave kings the justification for their titles.

First everywhere, winning, prevailing, going first.... On the balance sheet of his victories, his glory balances that of Christ, his account surpassed every fortune, his force prevailed over every power, and he legitimated every power. That is the new primacy of reason and science, masters of the world and men. Why did Majorana worry about an elevation and a power that filled his ancestor with joy?

Indeed, joy of the body, joy in the water, joy in the air. For the simple story of Archimedes's most famous discovery to have come down to us, unchanged, across two millennia of history, it must conceal a treasure.

Here's the naked engineer, in his bath. His floating body undulates, alone, in the volume like a toy boat in a small tub, where his limbs give themselves over to the slight rolling. A naked body, transparent fluid, a theorem of equilibrium by means of the waters: Archimedes feels the force that, by lifting him, causes him to float and swim.

I've found it, he yells, and there he is, come out, still naked, into the street, shouting and running in the agora, to the great astonishment of the stiff, draped, politic and standing people, who see without seeing, streaming with water and light, a body which dazzles me a second time with its truth value. Naked, like the day he came out of his mother's womb, and leaping like a child; naked, without any other apparatus, in the bath, on the ground and through the air, this body sinks but floats, stands and steps out of the water, walks, runs, leaving the tracks of its wet feet on the sand; finally, leaping with joy, takes flight, by following, in the air and wind, the *trouvaille*'s seraphic verb: *eureka*!

Eureka! I've felt, he says, the force of the wave that carries my body. But what second force makes it gush, now and in addition, out of the water? *Eureka*! I say, in turn, to generalize his theorem: every body honestly plunged into authentic life or into direct and courageous learning receives from them a force, equivalent to that of this body, directed upward, vertical, toward discovery. Invention makes the body fly, thus becoming archangelic. Spiritual. *Eureka*: how better to express the intoxication whose reason, happy, makes one float in the water and whose intuition, blessed, makes one levitate in the air? Archimedes felt the movement and rose with the emotion of these two elements, as though he heard the murmur of the waves and the vibration of the wind. And I hear *eureka* as this triple echo of body and air and water.

What story tells the *trouvaille*'s corporal joy with more plausibility? Thus, and again, he was the first, through the body, in the game of intelligent joy. Paradise.

Water, air. Earth, as a third. An engineer, he also knew how to build machines that no one had imagined before him. A sophisticated expert in winches and levers, Archimedes boasted a new Atlas, that he could lift the Earth; then, challenged, pulled and towed, with only one arm, a fully armed warship onto the sands of a beach by multiplying the forces through the intermediary of pulleys: he demonstrated it in front of the king surrounded by his court. Let reason show that it can dominate all things in this way with its force and who would be surprised that the princes of this world knock at its door to seek out its collaboration?

So they mobilized that indomitable power, the way men are raised for a battalion, with a view to that relentless fight for all control: war. Located in the center of the sea where the center of the lands said to be inhabited then were bathing, Sicily, rich and prosperous, was the object of appetites and conflicts. Indo-European Rome, to the north, was fighting against Semitic Carthage, to the south, and the tyrants of Sicily's Greek cities sometimes allied themselves with the one, sometimes with the other. To defend Syracuse, his rich and coveted city, Archimedes built heavy war machines, enormous towers from which levers launched projectiles at the enemy in order to destroy their ships.

Lifting the Earth, that's a wager, but also promotional swagger; pulling a ship with one arm, that's utility likely to relieve the difficulty of maneuvers, but also spectacle; launching projectiles, that's defending oneself, but also killing: three different results for a single theorem, the ratio of forces, and the corresponding machine, the beam – what a word! – of the lever. Can a principle be invented while controlling its consequences? Don't the lights of victory, by dint of wanting to win at the game of power and glory, blind us to the responsibilities of death? Two millennia ahead of time, Majorana's fears were already, step by step, coming to pass.

Water, air, earth. Fire, fourth and finally. By concentrating the Sun's rays by means of a curved mirror, Archimedes set fire from a distance. Before the Roman fleets, he erected gigantic mirrors shaped like those parabolas he knew so well, whose foci were set – How? We don't know – on the sails and hulls, which suddenly caught fire. In the middle of the open roadstead, a new Etna entered into eruption, fire in the water, and burned Metellus's vessels, the enemy general. Victory, the history books say.

Victory. The sailors burned like torches and screamed on the decks; the sails burned around the masts, crackling, and the flaming lava burned on the hillsides; the infant in his cradle burned and screamed. Victory. Men and women burned and screamed in the two Japanese ports twenty-three centuries later. Similar flames spread their ravages in the framework of fire and tears called history, the appalling history of victories, the appalling history of the dominant and the killers. When, in war, our own children burn and scream, we again sing victory to celebrate, along with history, the first or the strongest.

How did the light that shines in the middle of the mirrors in which women admire themselves and adorn their beauty produce these pyres? How did the thrilling joy of the *trouvaille*, which makes the finder's body levitate so highly, change into the clamor of death?

The battle raged in his native city. No one knows how Archimedes died. Yet the narratives agree. Did a Roman soldier, after the victory, kill him while he was attempting to solve a geometry problem, drawn, as was the custom, on the sand? Or: Metellus ordered that Archimedes be brought to him and the legionary who was looking for him called him by his name; absorbed, the geometer brushed him aside telling him not to mess up the diagram with his footsteps. The soldier, furious, ran him through with his sword; blood flowed over the problem; it effaced the drawing. Archimedes served fire, he died by fire. Or, it is also said, he was murdered by a soldier while bringing his astronomical instruments and engineering tools to the conquering general. Always first, continually victorious, a collaborator, he joined the camp of the victors, the only country he had ever known. Then, an anonymous person, a weak person, a sort of last person, neither rich nor powerful, made him disappear.

Some time later, Cicero, the celebrated lawyer of classical Rome, passing through Sicily, recounted, in Book V of the *Tusculanae*, that he searched for the tomb of the most illustrious scientist of the island amongst a tangle of briers and bushes, as though it too, like Majorana's later, had vanished.

I continue my tour of the world, of knowledge and men. From Catania to Palermo, the young Majorana, close to us, announced our anxieties concerning our knowledge; Archimedes, in Syracuse, ruled through the martial laws of master reason, which likes to think it's the first of men; he died from it. The last act of this tragic journey opens in the south of Sicily, where Empedocles signed the origin and started the legend.

Pascal called Archimedes the prince of geniuses; the word "prince," in truth, signifies the first. What could be more admirable than to invent or discover within a discipline, and to shout naked in the street: "I've found it!"? But more beautiful still: creating a science from nothing. Now, at the earliest dawn of our knowledge, one of these immense inaugurators lived in Sicily.

A continuer of Pythagoras, the legendary theorist of figures and numbers, himself a physicist, chemist, naturalist, doctor … at least using the titles of our specialist divisions, Empedocles counted, for the first time, the four *Elements*, which he called, in his Greek language, the roots of things, sowing. Everything, he said, comes from water, air, earth and fire, and everything returns there, after increase, decrease, exchanges and return to equilibrium. Since the sum of the first four numbers equals ten and since, for the

Pythagoreans, ten expresses the Universe, the four elements therefore form the world: that's one of the first laws, wholly archaic, of physics. But how do the four elements build the world?

Water, sea and river; earth, crevasses in the mountains; fire, volcanoes and calderas; air and atmospheric phenomena … those are the four elements, the very roots of things. But above all these are the principles that assemble and govern them: two contrary laws or forces work, mix, transform this quadruple sowing: love and hate. Not conceived like the emotions felt by the hearts and bellies of men and women, but like objective powers, that are free and mobile, they dominate things, both inert and living. Hate cuts, separates, distinguishes, dissolves, destroys, analyzes, scatters, kills … what love joins, unites, mixes, combines, constructs, harmonizes, causes to be born, grow and enjoy. Hate unleashes the enormous force that ties, through love, all things together.

Would they be called strong or weak interactions, attractions and repulsions today? No, for we no longer know how to see cyclones and sources, falls and births, winter, spring, the sunset and the dawn, the way he saw them, across that gigantic respiration whose alternation fragments and attaches, favors deadly brawls and happy coituses. To progress in the resolution of our anxieties, we would have to hear, once again, the thunder of our bombs as being emitted by Empedocles's two powers: an explosion of Hate driving back the peace of Love. And also to feel the world, noble but base, as well as life, cruel but generous, as subject to these two physical laws. Neither more nor less than ourselves.

By means of these element-dominating laws, this old physicist began to tear nature away from the ancient myths; by a strange return, today we're plunging our successes back into the anxieties and terrors from which that ancient physics was born. Yes, our new history of science and technology is plunging, today, as though in a loop, into the fundamental human myths from which Empedocles's first laws came. A major progression and a regression on the nether side of the origins. Consequently, the contemporary time requires that we try to return to that unity in which the principles of hate and love are at the same time human, living, inert and global. We will never attain a deontology of our knowledge and actions without thinking the subjective, the objective, the collective, and the cognitive all together simultaneously. Here, hate and love are the result of these four components.

The water-hate that refused Majorana, in which Archimedes, with love, bathed, became, for Empedocles, an element; likewise for the fire-hate that set Hiroshima ablaze, that Archimedes launched onto the Roman warships, and that Etna pours on their common island of Sicily. And, thirdly, the air-hate. A pestilential wind was blowing from the mountains, onto Agrigentum, killing the men and sterilizing the women; Empedocles made this blowing stop by plugging the passes and cured them.

One of the epidemics whose ravages, for centuries, decimated our ancestors so often, the plague – But what disease was meant by this name? – then broke out in Selinunte. The people of that city, neighboring Agrigentum, called for help from he whose theory and practices controlled, they believed, the elements. Empedocles observed then that the plague was spreading from the surrounding springs and backwaters. The Selinuntans were dying from dead water. Hate again. He, it is said, embarked upon civil engineering works that, by draining the swamps, reappropriated the reservoirs; some time after, the disease called a truce, to the enthusiastic relief of its victims.

All of Selinunte immediately invited the first master of the air, water, and earth to a religious and civil banquet where three of his elements returned, by him, from hate to love. The festivities lasted for a long time, for nothing pleases men's hearts like escaping death seen up close in one's immediate relations. The Selinuntans got drunk, no doubt, for they didn't see Empedocles slip away. The next day, no one saw him. And no one will ever find him again, as with Majorana later on.

Some said that he withdrew and died alone in Peloponnesus. But no one ever encountered him there. Others maintained that they saw him in glory, rising toward the heavens, become god; people told them they should stop drinking. The obscurity of his death therefore engendered a legend, similar to the one that, later, caught hold of Majorana, our elder brother in modern knowledge, and Archimedes, our first father in the ambitions of reason.

The most truthful version tells of his final journey and the end of his passion. He crossed the island from Selinunte to the foot of Mount Etna. A long walk: out of piety, Empedocles was wearing shoes of bronze to remove himself from earthly stains; a sign of immortality, that imperishable alloy separated the body, purified with love, from the hateful mud of the roads. How did he cross that long distance without anyone knowing it? Did he travel by night? Did he hide in the middle of the island, in the place said to be the "navel," where Persephone, abducted, entered into the Underworld? One might already think that his wandering no longer took place on the Earth, as though he as well had gone through a sort of boundary door.

He was meditating on the way. "To cure the women, children and men of the plague, I vanquished, through love, the hate of the foul waters, the hate of the pestilential winds, of the water-soaked earth or the parched soils. But what about, fourthly, the hate borne by the fire whose threat hangs over the island even more than over one of its cities? I know, like everyone, how to light this fire so that its love will warm us, but how to control its power when the eruptive blaze makes the air unbreathable and bombs the fields, evaporates the water and desolates our earth with nuclear hate?"

I insist on stressing the point. Empedocles didn't speak of love and hate as individual feelings only. He thought like those who, before our divisions, had no knowledge of our fragmentations. He saw, like Dante, what we don't see anymore, that love moves the Sun and the other stars.

Through weakness or anxiety, to be serious or for effectiveness, we no longer know how, we are no longer capable of speaking in any but disjointed terms, in special, specialized, specious discourses, as physicists or politicians, as historians or pious believers, through equations, poems or prayers, as scientists or those in love, in bad French or exact algebra. None of these discourses can or wants to rejoin the other, to encounter it, recognize it, yes, love it. We claim to hold colloquia, but we speak there in these dislocated terms.

Our analytical hate bursts into these little puzzle pieces, into these texts armored with compelling, aggressive, defensive citations. In fragmented lives, we think a world burst into technologies, sciences, separated languages. Our meaning lies in scattered limbs. By dint of quartering the subjective, the cognitive, the objective and the collective, how can we say the right word and live a happy life? The analysis that unties these four components comes from the hate that divides. What love will reunite them? That's the project of a thought, the program of a language, the hope of a life.

When Empedocles wrote about love and hate, he meant at once physics and society, the living body and the surrounding world, myth and knowledge, music and exactitude, moving emotion and untrembling rigor, my soft girlfriend and the implacable and precise hardness of things. I want to speak like him, at the global dimension of the world in which we live and think like guests.

I hear something like a unified voice burst forth from my triple narrative. My hope rests on the contemporary evolution of knowledge. Simple and easy, our old sciences rested on the analysis that separates and cuts up, on the cutting up that separates subjects from their objects. Hate? Difficult, global and connected, the life and Earth sciences presuppose communications, interferences, translations, distributions and passages. Love?

Let's understand as Empedocles understood it, the urgency of reuniting wisdom and knowledge, under penalty of collective eradication. He saw and makes us see that our history from its beginnings moves forward, like him, on the flanks of a volcano, closer and closer to the slash and burns of its crater.

He is now climbing its flanks. During the ascent of his calvary on molten Mount Etna, in the sweat of the effort and his deathly pain, Empedocles is approaching the mystery of the origins, of the big bang of world and human history, of the violence that separates and the energy that reunites things as well as humans. He is approaching the mouth of the volcano that destroys, through hate, the cultivable fields and, through love, causes the fragile relief of the Earth to be continually reborn.

Hard and triumphant like a mountain climb, the slow or rapid growth of knowledge requires an ascent just as vertical to a wisdom where a love, still unknown, would balance our essential compulsions of hate, exactly as the world shows and says such balance in its noises. Empedocles is climbing the flanks of the volcano in order to hear, through its violet mouth, the world say to him - *that*.

Three volcanoes and fires of hell, under the reign of hate: Majorana foresaw the flames of Hiroshima;

Archimedes built his scorching mirrors and the fleet, in front, exploded under the blazing fire; Empedocles, lastly, fell into the volcano; he hurled himself into Etna's crater.

In the incandescent caldera that our sciences prepared and caused to explode in the American desert and across the islands of Japan, we recognize a hellish hate that resides in and outside us, in our innermost consciousness and the social group, a hate that works and poisons our acts of knowledge, acts formerly written in myth, then in history and today in those technologies.

Empedocles vanished. He threw himself, it is said, into the molten crater. Was he looking, doubly, for those secrets of science and sapience? Did he want to listen as closely as possible to the voice of the hateful fire that burns and destroys and the voice of the power of love that combines atoms and makes things be born? For the legend claims that he believed in atoms, like many in Antiquity; it says, as well, that he threw himself into the crater and therefore returned to his elements, dissolved, decomposed into the mauve magma, but that, upon the morning of the next day, a sudden eruption threw his bronze sandals back, onto the rim of the crater. The volcano, the Biogea's vagina. Didn't Garonne, too, give birth to an island? Didn't the bergschrund, too, deliver Anne-Marie? Doesn't Mount Etna's crater yawn like the fissure of the Roman Forum? Like the opening between Bio, Empedocles's intense life, and Gea, his four elements? Like the life emerging from matter, by the same mysterious opening? At the rim of the burning abyss, like footprints, those shoes indicate at the same time where to come from and where to go. From where to be reborn. From and toward the originary place of the world where a deep organ voice rumbles. Gaping Mother Earth. Gaping Biogea.

Let's listen, there, to the screams of the Roman sailors that Archimedes burned, to the howls of Hiroshima's irradiated, whose torture the vanished Majorana no doubt wanted to avoid and prevent, or if not, delay; let's listen to the appeal sent out by Empedocles's vanished body, amid Etna's deafening thunder and tall flames … nothing but sobs emitted by men transformed into torches by fire.

No, Empedocles heard the dark mouth emit the sound of an enormous thing of the world, constructive of our planet and destructive of its landscapes, a voice bearing at the same time the rumblings of a crowd gone mad with conflict, the roaring of massacres, the insane suffering of sailors burning as though at the stake, the sobs of our passions and the warnings of our knowledge. He heard the noise common to personal appeal, to a human language, to a universal science, to an enormous thing of the world.

How to speak this voice? How to speak in several voices, that of things, that of knowledge, of emotions, of each and everyone, that of humanity? Will we, one day, by dint of listening to the voices of the Biogea, say this language? Like Aldo Leopold, Empedocles wanted to think like the mountain; to live like the earth on fire, the fire that warms with love and consumes with hate: to think like the elements of a science that was being born in its totality.

Like I would like to think.

Winds and
Atmospheric Phenomena

But who then writes history and selects the figures
worthy to enter into it? The great slaughters interest
us, the way to put an end to them much less so. Since
I've suffered many wars, I have sought, noiselessly,
peace. Thus, once and for that very thing, eighty
sailors, with me, ought to have figured in history.

Egypt's ruler around the 1950s, Colonel Nasser
one fine morning decided to nationalize the Suez
Canal. Having, then and since its digging, a major
financial interest in it, England and France sent, as in
the good old days, several gunboats to prevent what
they considered to be a theft. In the course of that
campaign, my sailor friends learned that the Cold
War perhaps amounted to a tragicomedy when they
saw the fleets, allied then, of the USSR and the United
States put themselves in the way of ours to try to stop

said intervention. Which ended in a rapid victory, just as quickly changed, as with the wars that were to follow, into a definitive defeat. So, encumbered with the wreckage of the sunken ships, the canal closed, in addition, to the passage of the colonialists.

Far from those outmoded fires, I was sailing on an escort in the Atlantic Squadron. One night, while I was on watch on the bridge, leeward of Iceland, by a moderate breeze and slight rain, the radio brought me a message from the Admiralty ordering me to return as quickly as possible to the port of Djibouti, where my new post was awaiting me on board an old military vessel, the *Adour*.

Cold-hot, pea coat left against the white cotton pants, there I was just to the south then of the Red Sea. The so-called old tub, broken in two, required lots of refitting, but since the mission was pressing – negotiating the reopening of the Suez Canal – we fixed its fragile hull with string. Having exploded from the bow on a beach in Indochina, it particularly lacked a prow and, at sea, moved like a duck. Exposed to a terrible heat wave, we went back up the Red Sea at the speed of a walking man, three knots. A tourist and forced observer, I would soon boast of knowing in detail the hydrography of those waters. Reaching Suez, anchored in the middle of the harbor, we displayed the signals meant for negotiation, as well as the white flag of peace. Cannons pointed at us,

Nasser's fleet first made a demonstration of strength around our vessel, completely disarmed. We saw ourselves condemned to become slaves at Aswan Dam, as in the time of the pharaohs.

After two days, a boat approached our side and the envoys of the government climbed aboard. Four men with potbellies, mustaches and big eyes, among which was their bald bespectacled leader wearing a rather dark three-piece suit, well-cut, bright polished shoes and a red tie – all of them marvelously French-speaking – entered the wardroom where the skipper, in full evening dress, with his decorations hanging, surrounded by his chief steward and his officers, to which I belonged, offered them champagne, cakes and cigars; "Smiles, gentleman, you will be staying for dinner." Needless to say that, for our part, we were prepared for subtle diplomacy, for a refined game of sophisticated arguments intended to have the canal reopen to our ships without making too many concessions. When is the palaver going to begin? We were on our guard.

The four sat down in the armchairs, lit cigars, sipped from their glasses. With a broad laugh and a friendly accent, the fat brown-haired one with glasses declared out of the blue: "You pay, you pass."

Never was I so disappointed. At once, the admiration I had contracted at school for high authorities of power evaporated in my head. Were these things then so easy? My soul never knew how to re-inflate this old soufflé that had fallen then. Facing sentimental enemies, we no longer talked about anything but money and the weather, perhaps also about children. The wardroom filled with bawdy stories. For a long time I've regretted not having kept the addresses of these friends of a moment, likeable and pudgy.

So we paid; we set sail. It remains to be said that the passage through the canal quickly turned into an infernal nightmare. The old pilots had fled the war or the risk of prison; those who replaced them, inexperienced, had never navigated in these narrow and peculiar waters, in which each tonnage posed singular problems of holding course and squat effects; we risked gigantic accidents a thousand times. I remember having come within a millimeter of a humongous Greek oil tanker: the pilots hadn't seen each other! We had to steer without them, against their advice, all the while filling them up with champagne to make them forget their blunders.

We only breathed easy at Port Said. Yet my narrative is only beginning; what had just happened being only old history. For from the forked mooring to the port, it seemed to me that an era – outdated, overrun with dinosaurs – was coming to a close. As we embarked toward the Mediterranean, dozens of the red cockroaches that, enormous, infested the ship in a tropical climate, came out from everywhere under the quickwork so as to come and die on the deck in the colder open air. And the black cockroaches reappeared, smaller. Were they reborn? We were changing living species at the same time as epoch and latitude. Again the swing from an old history to another. I'm going to quickly say that I changed age as well, at the same time as the epoch, profession, thought, future, world, and sea. The reopening of the canal gave birth to a new me.

Port Said was disappearing at the southern horizon; we were heading, diagonally, for the first seamark southeast of Crete. The season must be told: December. None of us was a practiced pilot for the eastern Mediterranean in winter. We should have known and we didn't. It didn't dawdle. From the first night watch, a first giant wave covered the ship. It no longer stopped. Three hours later, another, even higher, swept away the radio unit from which we'd already sent out distress calls: mayday! It has to be told that we had, in Djibouti, loaded a cruiser propeller of colossal dimensions, secured in the hold, and which could, by tearing out its moorings, cut fatal leaks into the hull and below the waterline.

Panic on board. Quell it first; the doctor himself was screaming with fear while running in the gangways and was risking bringing about collective madness. Aided by two sailors, I had to give him a good shot in the buttocks so he would sleep; I'd never given anyone whatsoever a shot before, I haven't done it since. Sea Ten. How many sick? Many. How many available. Few. The thing lasted five nights and six days.

First, the noise. We no longer heard each other. As we were trying to hold course, the wind would modulate its howling according to the height of the wave, straight in front, like a building of several stories: becalmed, in the trough; gusting hard, at the crest. The commotion of this variation would mix with the vagaries of the fractal fracas of the waves and the sinister creaking of the boat. Yes, I heard the Biogea, that day of wrath. Blowing, howling, raging.

Next, the motion. The rolling would force us to walk on the port bulkhead, then stand upright on the floor, after that jump onto the starboard wall. Every minute. Lastly, survival. Impossible to sleep and eat. In one's left pocket, a round loaf; in the right, a flask of port. For big storms, I recommend this divine wine. I held out by means of bread fingers. Long live the Portuguese, old sailors before the Lord.

In Paris one morning, my wife received a telephone call from the Admiralty gently asking her to be prepared for the worst. "Have you had any news from the midshipman? We haven't had any." Fortunately, she didn't understand a thing about this message and thought there must be some error. So the only suspense was for the seafaring people who, for their part, knew that a six-day radio silence meant a loss of all resources and human contact.

Every minute, we did indeed await the end. We knew that this old tub patched up with string couldn't survive such a storm. It's in God's hands! I testify that a kind of calm comes over the soul at these limits. Far from impeding them, exceptionally savage conditions, on the contrary, help a crew who's confined to looking after the ship the way doctors do a dying man. With softness in the hardness, joy in the tempest, serenity before the event. All the more peaceful because the end was imminent. The relations among ourselves became those that I knew, long after, roped together on demanding rock faces. Perfect, ecstatic even. Do you want to know love? Face Sea Ten in company, small in number, but growing in esteem!

Death, seen up close, felt, perceived, experienced in the closest proximity. Again one corpse or several. What is of interest in this story? The nearness of shipwreck, the probable drowning, the struggle with death, the possibility of dying? No, again, no and no.

I repeat what I've said and continue the lesson. For, once more, who died shortly after? Not the crew, not the sailors, not anyone. Driven from the western point of Crete to the waters of Haifa, as soon as the wind had – relatively – calmed, we steered again on our due west heading, ending by recognizing, around Pantelleria, a tub that was looking for us, worried because they hadn't received us on time at the quay of Bizerte. Saved. Living. Surviving: above life; since then, I've been living differently. Standing with pride from having honorably ridden out the wind. And we were closely related to Saint Paul who, in the Acts of the Apostles, recounted a similar heavy blow in these waters. And to Nelson as well, who said he had undergone a similar terror there. And Ulysses, too, why not? Proud of this high kinship. Like these immortals, we didn't die those days.

THE SEA'S TOMB

But the sea is dying, the sea is dead. We're killing the sea the way we are the rivers. Foul waters, dying fish, the depths scraped by trawl nets and then saturated with garbage. As well as the idiotic tourism of the rich, coastal, pseudo-scientific, deep-sea, pleasure-boating … as well as the media entertainers whose ten helicopters soil the air and water so as to condemn, by means of striking images, this filth. The womb of all specific life is dying. How many aquatic and terrestrial species are dying every day? What crew of solitary sailors will set sail, tomorrow, on the cemetery seas? Hell.

Who thinks like the dying sea? What writer, other than Homer or Conrad, thinks like the wind?

Who has quite as much spirit as the pleasant breeze that makes our fragile hull dance so? Yes, my permanent tinnitus causes me to hear the wind's clamor again, at the time of my entry, with a pretty fanfare, into a new life. The breeze howled, then, with menace. It's crying today in supplication. We sent out our distress calls in the days when the sea still dominated us. The game has turned. The wind now calls for help. I can no longer hear the surf or the hurricane without deciphering those canonic calls: mayday, help me, come help me!

Oh, sailors, old comrades, you formerly had the mission of defending the nation at sea, a supremely noble calling. You now have defending the sea as your mission. Against whom? Against ten others, no doubt, but also sometimes against your own nation. Yes, the sea is dying, the sea is dead! Do you want to wander tomorrow on dead oceans? Make the sea be reborn.

The Sun's Tomb

At the end of his *Divine Comedy*, Dante wrote, as Empedocles would have done, that Love moves the Sun and the stars: the three can disappear. And die like the rivers, the Earth and the sea.

Less a quarter of an hour before the eclipse, at noon, a mass of clouds, stable for four days, persuaded me to give up on observing the event: the Sun and Moon went absent. Prepared for that contingency, frequent with these types of phenomena, I went up to pack my bags when a cry outside made me come back down: a miracle, the thick clouds withdrew; driven by a wave of wind, a paintbrush of strangeness separated the mass, and the spectacle began. Rebirth in the opening.

I readily admit that every partial eclipse is banal; thin or thick, the Sun's crescent resembles then, with more brilliance, our usual monthly moon; furthermore, the smallest of its parts still gives out daylight. Indefinitely divided, God or the infinite remain infinite. Of course, a shadow covers the Earth; but, there again, who hasn't lived through such twilights? At sunset, the horizon indeed masks the Sun.

Everything happens, then, during the seconds of complete veiling. Hardly had it begun than a strange light, yellow and tawny, resembling nothing else, neither the evening nor the dawn, invaded the environment; the glory of orange light intercepted by the walls of my abode disappeared, giving way to a somber and magic bath, which I'm not surprised had frightened certain of our ancestors; the littlest of the children who were present took refuge in the house and his mother, later, acknowledged her terror, whose pregnancy I in turn am trying to describe. During the short moments of this pallid noon, I understood what darkness, in the singular, meant. Not the total black, but a bizarre night, with a dull glow within; our beautiful nights also glimmer inwardly, but like the heart of a diamond. Everything, there, became pale and drab in a way different than under creamy moonlight: this flatness without honey or milk may explain the funereal impression produced by the event. Without the Sun, death presents itself in person, dull and dismal. Mourning: the world dies.

But, assuredly, the most sublime comes from the fitting of one celestial body over another, leaving its corona radiating around. Closing of the open. Everyone has seen the photographs, but direct vision of it, without goggles, scorches. What I said about light is then repeated for color. Hiding the solar rays, the Moon becomes achromatic. Even if, in general, the visible is tinted then, nothing is colored anymore, neither yellow, nor tawny. This neutrality may again explain the funerary impression produced by this mourning veil. No culture, across the world, expresses death by means of a color: in black or in white, or in white and black, without brilliance or value.

Never does one see that; admittedly, it's a matter of a rarely visible thing; but, in addition, it breaks up the exercise of vision. Never does one see like that: neither that object, nor in so flat an atmosphere, nor by means of the undone gaze. Whoever has known the joy of a revelation would no doubt grasp what could be named, conversely, "velation" or veiling:

privation of obviousness and jubilation. The strange silence bathing the darkness also approached this apperception, very well-named for once: never does one hear like that. No, neither silence nor deafness ever reigns like that. Does hearing also depend on thermal waves spread from the Sun? Was I shivering? I was cold to the point of putting on a sweater and a wool sweat suit. Never had I felt things nor myself like that … like the child taking refuge or the anxious mother. Frozen, the body lets itself be ejected outside its immersion in sensation, sensation that, on the contrary, assures survival if it leaves this specter outside it.

I haven't looked at the Sun in the same way since. Without source, father, mother or life, I lived outside the world for that endless minute in which, worse than death, absolute absence occurred. This abandonment resembled the loss of a love.

Hell on Earth.

Hymn to the Paradise of the Green Ray
Over endless days, as I was just recounting, we went back up the Red Sea from Djibouti to Suez at three knots, the speed of a walker. A hundred men in a falling apart iron hull beneath a devil of a sun, an exquisite torture. Over endless nights, the heat wouldn't abate. We threw buckets of salty water on our bunks, the engineer officers would fight in the

hold, drunk, and the bakers refused to relight their hellish ovens.

The cliffs that, sometimes, run alongside this sea stood out in narrow vertical slices of such different heights that, when seen from the open sea, made us believe they were minarets overlooking the lower buildings of a city interrupted by breathtakingly high skyscrapers. In the desert's place stood, in facade and depth, a dream city, gigantic, set with palaces from *One Thousand and One Nights*. Columns emanating from evaporation, intense and – here and there – variable, explained the optics of these illusions.

The *Instructions nautiques* asserted that a lateral current caused the ships to drift in one direction in the morning and in another in the evening. As we were crawling along for a long time in these waters, we supposed that these zigzags amounted to aberrations analogous to the cliff-cities. The correctness of this hypothesis was revealed by observations, with the sextant, of a probable mirage that would lower and then raise the horizon, combined with precise calculations. We sent our assessment later to the Naval Hydrographic Service, which rectified the error.

Amid these evil spells, we saw the green ray twenty times. I only saw it again one evening six decades later in the Iroise Sea, at the opening of the *Tas de Pois*. A red disk, the Sun was going down; a crimson semi-circle; a ruby quarter of a circle; a still scarlet tenth of a circle. When it reached – oh, paradox – the size of a lune, then, from that quasi punctual source, yes, abstract like an aperture, deep as a tunnel, shot out a light I have never enjoyed since: a column jet of round emerald with an intense light, a dense brightness, a straight irradiation of a full serpentine, a supernatural purity of vivid olivine. Thus, better than dazzled, the vision fulfilled sight, the way food can appease or a lover satisfy.

Among the infernal living conditions, pain, thirst and misleading illusions, did the green ray tell us, by canal or aperture, of a narrow door for being reborn into paradise?

Flora and Fauna

BURNING RATS

We read maps, like every page, from left to right. Thus, we sweep France with our eyes from Finestère to Kehl. I therefore know the first lady of France; when I arrive from the open sea, on land or on the map, I see her house. I can't miss it, solitary, the first on the northwest point of the Island of Ushant. With the lighthouse keeper of Créac'h, she previously formed a community of islanders allied with the west wind, whose dominating voice had taught more about itself to them than to anyone else, sailors included.

Créac'h? Oh, do I remember lighthouses! When they became museums for indifferent tourists, I thought I'd fallen off the snows of yesteryear. Yes, within sight of the coastline, we used to navigate, anxious, with one eye on their flashes or their occultations, and the other on one of the *Lights and*

Fog Signals, works lined up, on the shelves of the bridge, in a special row: *Series A, Mediterranean*; *Series B, Atlantic*, etc. Anxious, since a hundred sailors were sleeping beneath our feet, we nevertheless couldn't go wrong, each turn having its name, its gleams, its bearing and its site. Those lights behind which strangers in whom we had confidence were on duty made me prefer a night watch, even amid the shallows and congested sea lanes, to those of the day. Treacherous, the light; safe, the darkness.

Among the last of the keepers, old Arhan, the lord of Créac'h, a giant tower on the west end Ushant, was going to take an early retirement since his trade was dying, replaced by electronics. Instructed, like every solitary, he loved to chatter about his monastic years the way sailors recount stories about ghost ships. That first lady of the West of mine was evidently a welcome visitor at the lighthouse, where the keeper continually recounted stories to her.

This one, for instance:

"Just as alone in his hermitage as yours truly, but miles from here, madam, south of us, in that strange Mediterranean devoid of tides, a colleague keeping watch off Vulcano Island, in the Aeolian Islands, also known as the Lipari, not far from the shores of Sicily, I'm talking about the days of the wooden navy and about places I imagine without ever having sailed there, a colleague, as I was saying, one fine morning saw, while he was tranquilly cleaning the lenses of his lamps with a shammy in his lantern room, an ugly dismasted hull come straight toward his rock. He gestured, shook his handkerchief, to no avail; the boat, holding course, came closer, closer…. My colleague rushed down the spiral staircase four at a time, took down the semaphore signs at a run, left by the door onto the rock, and unfurled all he could of the green, red and turquoise blue surface so that the imbeciles would turn as quickly as possible. 'My word, everyone on board is drunk,' he said to himself."

"He, my colleague, was the imbecile, when he realized, but then quite late for his ignorant landsman skin, that it was a matter of what was called in those days a ghost ship, not that of the Wagnerian circus, but of those unfortunate boats on which the crew was no longer able to reason with the small beasts and on which, entirely in reverse, said beasts feasted on the organs and bones of all the sailors, including the skipper and the ship's boy for dessert. It even sometimes happened that a few last survivors lowered the whaleboat and left the rodents as the sole masters of the ship. Every man for himself! And here came the hull invaded by four-legged sailors with mustachioed snouts and pink tails drifting with the winds and in God's hands. In those days, lookouts from every ship would steer clear of them, crossing themselves, when they encountered those ill-fated boats from afar."

"Come on, Monsieur Arhan, you exaggerate. I don't believe in ghost ships."

"At the time of my Navy service, I myself saw, on land, a poor quartermaster, on guard in a sort of fallout shelter, come out one morning quite injured. A power failure had locked him in the cellar for the night, the airtight doors blocked by the automatic locks. Blindly and barehanded, for twelve solid hours he had to fight those beasts from hell, certain of which would jump on his face, attacking his soft parts and eyes, while others ate his calves. Fortunately, they weren't very numerous. A swarming pack would have devoured him before midnight, completely raw. He spent two months in Morvan hospital."

"I'm getting back to my boats. When the hellish new passengers no longer had anything for their teeth to gnaw on – hawser, barrel, dried cod, biscuits or sailors – they would end up, starving, dying with open mouths, rabid, or by killing each other so as to eat one another, like cursed shipwrecked people. We kill one another, you know, madam, us and the rats, the only animals that murder within their species."

"You know," said old Arhan with a nervous motion of his pipe, "when there's no longer anything but humans on the Earth, like the rodents of the lighthouse and boat, when we've destroyed every other living species, at the rate that this disaster is going today, who'll eat what, I ask you, aboard our ghost planet? We'll devour each other between brothers and sisters on this cursed ship. And drink the blood of our cousins. When is it due to arrive?"

"I am getting back, madam, to my Italian lighthouse. Letting go, at once, of the whole load of pennants, my colleague bolted flat out to lock himself in his stone tower at the very moment that this yacht of rotten wood crashed with a great noise on the lighthouse rocks – the entire rest of his life, the keeper heard, after this fracas of shattered sterns, the immense rumbling of the rats whose enraged mob cries drowned out, at a stroke, the background noise made by the sea, even calm – and that tens of thousands of animals, fasting since forever and a day, rushed and disembarked all together, like a syzygy tide flowing at Mont Saint-Michel, and galloped at his heels to devour him, pea coat included. He went through the door, didn't have time to close it, didn't succeed under the weight of the invasion in barricading it, climbed the steps fast as the wind with these millions of creatures at his heels, already trampling them, crushed two or three, finally reached the lantern room, slammed the iron leaf behind him, slid the three bolts, and, before collapsing with breathlessness and terror, battered with a bar the five or six intruders that succeeded in penetrating with him all the way upstairs into the glass cockpit of the lantern room. End of the first act."

"Scene now. A pretty sea, gentle wind, spring clouds, booms and ratlines broken in disorder at the lighthouse's foot, and the entire hillock islet now covered with this moving swarming, of an innumerable depth, and above all – oh, my eardrums – the enormous rumbling of the rodents attempting to climb the tower, covering almost all of it, filling at least the totality of the volume of the spiral staircase…. Was the door of the lantern going to hold? Howling and sticky, a mass was pushing it and, behind the fragile panel, my poor colleague panting. That, madam, is the entire story: all of a sudden, without warning, alone against an army. You think you're calm, cleaning your things with a nanny-goat skin, and, suddenly, the downpour of rats…. Who'd believe it?"

Through the whistling of the west wind that enveloped Créac'h like a flapping tunic, while said first lady was having coffee in the watch room, she thought she heard the shrill commotion of that appalling mob seeking to devour everything.

"The second act, Monsieur Arhan?"

"Scene, again. From the harbor master's residence on land, at Milazzo I believe, without being able to guarantee it, it was of course impossible to see, in the evening, out in the open sea, the flashes of the lighthouse. Stuck next to the lenses, hungry, thirsty, without sleep due to fright, my colleague couldn't light the lamp: the sparking device was outside the lantern room, on the side with the rats. Who, from the Sicilian shore, could have guessed the adventure? The officials raged, saying that the keeper was failing in his duties. 'Is the bastard drunk?' 'No, sick,' said his substitute colleagues, better-speaking than those slanderers. And the lighthouse remained in the dark. Navigation became dangerous again in the region, and the Strait of Messina sea lane – Charybdis and Scylla, madam! – wasn't far from there. Something had to be done quickly, for no arriving ship could know that the signal had gone out. No AVURNAV at that time, nor radio or Internet, nor that infernal GPS that could, certainly, lead us to paradise."

"At the end of the night of waiting, still hoping that the keeper would relight, they fitted out some dingy or other to go and have a look on the scene. And they saw, yes, the leaning, ripped-open wreck, almost upright on the rock, the foremast fallen across, the beam demolished, the boom broken, in the midst of scattered planks; and on the aft wall: *Danae*, from Liverpool." "No!" exclaimed old Arhan, "my colleague's tower didn't receive a shower of gold that morning, but a flood of cries! For they also saw, no, rather heard, the infernal pullulating; the lighthouse moving with life and vibrating with deafening howls. I have difficulty believing what the witnesses said on their return: the rats, having climbed clutching one over the other, were piled up along the tower and were forming, outside, from top to bottom, up to the lantern room to which they couldn't hoist themselves without slipping, a kind of colossal vibrating column, howling to the skies from starvation."

"Impossible to disembark, as you can imagine. They crossed themselves, the way the lookouts who passed that horror formerly did on the open sea; they returned to land and wondered what to do. What would you have done, madam? What would I have done myself to fight against that tide, to defeat the invincible armada?"

Arhan left the first lady of France in suspense for a moment.

"The third and final act?" she said.

"Then, the stroke of genius: I no longer know which quartermaster, the son of a butcher from the neighboring village on the coast, rushed into the harbor master's in the morning, shoved the guard aside, and, stuttering his sentences, so much were the words crowding against his teeth, suggested that a tugboat should set sail at once ('An idea my little sister had,' he said, 'you know, the piquant brunette, the one in love with the keeper, who'd so much like to marry him.') with a barge crammed with bones and rotting meat in tow. His father would get them at the renderer and bring them right away with the horse. The harbor master, understanding nothing of all this, considered the sailor crazy, but embarked with him on the barge. Everything had to be tried."

"They got underway to the ghost lighthouse; arriving within sight of it, they maneuvered in circles, slowly, so that the barge, at the end of the towline and full to bursting with the remnants of the rendering, would land, in its turn, by gently hitting the rocks; it touched them, caressing them with its quarter on land. Drawn, lured, intoxicated by the abominable odor of meat as infernal as their rabidity, the rats, seeing the end of their Ramadan, undressed and emptied the lighthouse in a lightning-fast stampede, hurtling down the stairs, freeing the islet, racing in carnage to the boat and, piled on, filled it to the brim at the risk of sending it to the bottom. Then, the quartermaster, having a quiet laugh, cut the cable, and the rats, mustaches, paws and mouths red with the blood of the rotting meat, became the sailors of a second ghost ship, wandering once again with the wind and on the pretty sea. Onto which the tug's pumps then poured tons of gas in a stream."

"'Take the torch, sailor, and set fire to those pests, God dammit!' 'I too remember,' recounted later the owner of the tug and barge, having shouted that order, 'I remember the infernal clamor emitted by that swarming and scorched city, plunged in crimson flames that shot up, instantaneously, as high as the lighthouse. Fanned by a gust of wind, the giant and reeking fire ship drifted out into the open sea for a long time; vanishing behind the horizon, in front of the setting sun, one would have thought it a second erupting Stromboli. The girl in love had a good idea. Love doesn't only move the stars, it also lights volcanoes.'"

"They plied the oars toward the lighthouse, where they picked my colleague, gone mad, up off the floor of the lantern room. For a long time, he remained in an asylum where his ears still resonated with the innumerable rumbling of the rats pushing in mass behind the shaky bolts ready to come loose."

"For a long time he didn't dare open when someone was knocking at his door."

From that day on, the lady of the waterside feared seeing the rebirth, come from the western horizon and making for her, of a ghost swarming with little beasts.

ANOTHER DISEMBARKATION

The squadron berthed with the evening low tide. The marines disembarked. Mines, grenades, corpses, fearsome explosions of fire. Now, the following night, rats – acrobats scurrying and balancing along the taut or slack hawsers – surreptitiously left the ships, invading the shores, dark cellars, and even the surrounding farms. No one noticed it; they only saw the army, in large numbers; they only heard the cannonade, deafening. Later, even more discreetly, twenty fleas jumped from each rat's fur and spread out into the rooms, closets, sheets, clothes, and body hair. So secretly that it took millennia to understand its behavior, *Pasteurella pestis*, leaving the fleas in turn, its clouds filled up with ten minuscule interstices among the organs and blood of the living.

Relating the disembarkation, history and the newspapers announced thousands of deaths. But what do the soldiers and their theater blunderbusses weigh next to the morbidity of these little microbes? In the final accounting, the most decisive slaughter took place during the final stage of that quadruple arrival, unfolding like Russian dolls. Not to mention that said boats discharged ballast near the coastline and that the waters they released spread ten other deadly species. The most lethal bombs? These sources of plague, whose infections have always brought about more death than wars. In spite of our boasting, even directed toward our most vile acts of violence, despite our sublime talents as murderers, we're not as good as the rats and the fleas, nor the bacteria and viruses. Except quite recently, when our last conflict killed – victory! – more men and women than these beasts.

Evident result: tiny causes sometimes have more effects than perceptible ones. What to say, then, about testimony, observation, experience? What are hearing, sight, good sense worth? What do our histories, blind, say that is true? Yes, newness arises, invisible beneath our empty spectacles, like thieves, noiselessly, at night. I shall soon have to say that at the extreme end of a ladder whose rungs become thinner, the soft decides better than the hard.

Sailors, rats, fleas, microbes … but also ants and other insects, seaweed or plants, we call these species: invasive. Dynamic, expansive, their populations readily flood the world. And, before their advance, encounter others, similar, uncontrollable for their part as well. Hence fierce competition, like that which formerly flamed between sailors and rats on ships. Which species, finally, uniquely victorious, will reign on this ship … on this island I call the Biogea? What will happen if one species, ours for instance, prevails? Who will it eat then, if not its fellow men? I hear old Arhan grumbling into his pipe again.

How then do we control the propagations of these living things, small, swarming, often caused by our own transportation? How do we avoid a hundred wars between ourselves, first between invasive tribes, the Romans in Antiquity, the Huns under Attila, the French of the Napoleonic Wars, the English on the seas and in languages, colonialists, Nazis, Stalinists, multi-national companies … all thus fallen to the rank of viruses or stinging jellyfish? How do we avoid, next, a hundred wars between these species, between several anthills, for instance, and a hundred wars, again, between them and us, as in the lighthouse? Do we have to kill each other, burn or destroy one another, like the barge's sailors did?

Once again, we're on the same level as the other living things. Yes, among the most invasive species, we're one of the lively ones; neither more nor less than ants, seaweed or rats. Invading the Biogea for thousands of years, our hunting, gathering, cultivations, breedings, cities, industries and transportations … continually disrupt vital local balances by favoring, in addition, the disembarkation of other species, just as invasive as we are.

Once again, we cannot claim to be subjects in the midst of a world of objects, for our behavior resembles that of other insects, other rodents or poisonous plants. Not separated, but plunged, immersed in the Biogea, in cousin company. I want to think like that company, in it, by it, with it, for it.

Warning! We can no longer resolve ourselves to this war of every man against every man, fatal in the final analysis to the entire Biogea and consequently to us. Peace. Would a new Eden emerge if we agreed to a Natural Contract?

Which? Drawn up in what language?

Beware. Language, even the most insane cries, spread in front of and around them by the invasives, themselves become invasive. It suffices to descend the levels of the ladder again, at the disembarkation of just now: soldiers, rats, fleas, microbes, living things of more and more tenuous size and power, then on the nether side of these single-celled organisms, below the molecule, behind the atom … to cross the barrier of the hard, entropic, and reach information – which I just called soft – calls, signs, language. They can expand the same way in time and space.

Thus advertisements, images and words, thus victories, triumphs, glories, expansive successes of all stripes, imitate epidemics, the latter caused by the reproduction of those minuscule animals, the former by the trumpets of fame: printing, web, media … invasion-making machines. The multiple horror of billboards at city entrances reproduces, in nauseating ugliness, the cacophonous conflicts declared by these squawkers. Our bodies suffer, in return, from the signals that we scatter in this way. Would it consequently be surprising if, for example, the fast-food establishments, whose logos and displays are spread everywhere in the world, spread diseases like obesity, where the body, invasive in turn, spreads across space?

But neither do we have to pride ourselves on having invented the invasive via the soft. Look.

Another invasive species, wolves cross Asia in packs, from the north to the south, pass through the Gobi and the mountains, haunt the forests and circle around farms during winter. From the dawn of time, we've feared and told stories about these fabulous animals because they resemble us, in cruelty, prudence and cynicism, strategy, politics and pedagogy; we've given their name to the Louvre, our Council Rock, and to the secondary schools, in which we try to counsel the children of man. In the story of her life, George Sand recounts that she heard their great howling at night in the forest of the Landes, terrified under the covers of her conjugal bed, where, tranquil, her Dudevant of a husband was snoring. The pack was howling in its parliament. Parleying in its howling?

The meaning that sometimes emerges from the world's background noise bursts forth better from their maws than from floods, storms and volcanoes. I've heard wolves crying louder than the lighthouse rats.

You have to climb higher, indeed, than old Taciturn's Mount Ararat or Empedocles's Mount Etna to risk dying from damp sweat. Doctor Étienne, of glorious memory, who reached the North Pole on foot, recounted, with his modest gaiety, that he owed this exploit to a brush. In the cold of those regions, beard and fur quickly become sharpened with ice needles, and he said in the evening, if you enter the igloo you've just modeled without having first and carefully rubbed these hairs bristling like pendants, all of it will melt during the night and you'll never rid yourself of those puddles. Never dry, you die from the cold.

Ignorant of Étienne's high knowledge, I've spent, in a tent on the ice, painful nights shivering with all my limbs on the Lukla path to Everest. Sleep eluded me under the whistling of the north wind, to which was added, in a higher score [*partition*], the chattering of the jackals and the howling of the wolves barred, in a lower key, by the barking guard dogs. I insist on the term *partition*, whose meaning seems to associate what is separated. *Tutti*: were these animals fighting, threatening, tuning up? I regretted then not composing, after the manner of Messiaen, in order to hear better by reproducing it, the set of the messages carried by this black night's din. I don't remember ever having heard by day such a cacophonous orchestration. Do lights, the Sun, extinguish the emergence of meaning?

Meaning? The wind spreads by means of variable waves, by means of beats and interferences: thunders, explodes, vibrates, whistles high, sounds low, makes the entire world enter into its intense, regular and chaotic trance: on the sea, whips up waves, elsewhere lays the palm trees flat; here changes the place and swelling of the dunes; there carries everything away, takes flight, and covers you with avalanches of sand; its tarrying will leave the beach covered with flotsam, the dirty sea covered with gray spray and the desert pavement reshaped. Its breath, thus, binds its arrhythmic rhythm to the chaos of its light gusts, its direction to its disorder and the sound to the background noise.

Thanks to the wind and through it, I think I understand how a language begins. We too start from the commotion triggered by an emotion in the groin and translate it by means of vocalizations, laments and cries into disjointed waves and jerky rhythms accompanied by showers of sobs. The mouth opens and frees from the howling of the wind; do the wind's lips, conversely, blow with emotions?

In those mountains preceding the true Himalayan peaks, do you remember, my ropemate, that it was indeed twice a question of a score? A musical score strings together several clefs, C, F or G, one above the other, for several instruments, violins, clarinets, bassoons. Here: at the bottom, crackled, on the tent, the grapeshot of snow or hail brought by the wind that made the canvas flap; above, the jackals, hoarse, and the wolves, of high tessitura; finally the dogs, later I'll say a few humans. At the bottom, the background noise, the chaos of things whose broken parts blow away and scatter so as to lie, afterwards; above, the thunder, explosions and breakings; next, the highs and the lows, vibrating, therefore rhythm, still very irregular, but already meaningful.

"Listen to those cries and the baying of the dogs," whispered my companion in the tent. No, listen now to the great howling of the wolves. Magnificent, almost sublime, emanating from vertical legs placed in a triangle on the ground and from a mouth lifted straight toward the sky, already strangely musical. No, listen, there, uglier, raw, as though broken, to the chattering of the jackals. No, there, now, to the whistling of the wind. No, even here, to the ice and flying dust crackling together on the canvas of the tent. Incapable of analyzing them, did we understand these mixtures composed like Fourier sums?

Who or what cried more loudly than the others? The shrill whistling of the wind, the grapeshot of the hail, the three varieties of baying? Which invasive calls will stop the invasive calls from elsewhere, from others, from there, from here? Before the orchestra, before the score, before the contract for harmony, the nocturnal pandemonium of the jungle declared, loudly, the war in vortices of waves against waves.

Thus, put in place as best it could, a novice orchestra was executing what couldn't yet pass for a composition, but whose construction, unbuilt, rebuilt, reinforced our disappointed expectation and destroyed my rest, destroyed the attention of my female friend and bolstered our insomnia. One might rather have said, false and apt, a rehearsal: *prova d'orchestra*. The noise begins the rhythm that smooths out the noise; the rhythm erases the noise that destroys the rhythm. Were our emotions born from these arrhythmic movements?

The same goes for the narrative I would like to recount inspired by these breaths of wind. One would follow the rhythmic sequences of my story, but attention would collapse through the disordered breaks of this furious tempo, to resume, concentrated, fascinated, when another rhythm would be reborn. A rapid and linear order; then suddenly disorder, coup de théâtre, repercussion. Like the eddying wind. Running wind astern, my narrative would have some yawing about. Yet, if I only tell of the wind, who could be interested in what I say there? The wind doesn't speak by means of its violence, but it nevertheless sets at the same time the tone and the tempo, a tempo interrupted with disharmonies, the ruptures of rhythm. The entire exact program of a sustained interest, but without any meaning. And yet I would like to say here the first grain of meaning carried by the spirit of the wind, the one that blew on the confusion.

What were you saying, my ropemate friend, or better, here, my vibrating string friend? Ah, who was speaking? No one and nothing of all that spoke or had any meaning. Except, precisely, the invasive struggle, the threat, the fear, a rumbling whose intensity caused in us, the way the thunder of an earthquakes does, an intense anxiety in the belly and the awareness that our existence, paltry, timid, fragile, could vanish at any moment. Indeed, all of this had no meaning, except the emotion aroused by these grandiose sounds. But the emotion which trembled in our guts vibrated in a way that resembled the north wind's whistling and the wolves' howling, the wolves that were scared of the dogs, that were feared by the jackals and that yelped to drive back those carnivorous devourers of lambs guarded by women who were, in turn, calling. I heard the acoustic frequency of the noises, outside, the way I did that acoustic frequency which, within, shuddered and shivered in my chest and made me quake at the knees. How would we defend our tent if the pack of wolves besieged it? In the dark, I saw their open maw, and I heard them howl.

Mundus patet: the world opens. The jackals' and wolves' jaws opened. *Ego pateo*: I opened to the terror of the world. Which was shuddering with terror: me or it? Interfering, we both vibrated together, like the canvas of the tent and the wind, with fear, with emotions, with similar movements. The world was trembling with fear and shouted that fact out; we were shaking with anxiety, my companion and I, and we confided it to one another, in silence, to build up some courage together. Weak, fragile, vibrating in the wind, the tent's canvas sang, it too, its anxiety and the tranquility of its fragile courage.

What I'm recounting – those nights of terror for two in the Himalayan cold – is of no interest, as I've said, because it lacks meaning. But what meaning carried by what word and, first, what vocalization would ever have rung in the ambient air if the moans of the wind, the yelping of some jackal, the great howling of some pack, the barking of the dogs defending the farms … had never preceded the birth of language? The silky murmur of Garonne, the thunderstorms in the Alps and the Mediterranean, the thunder of earthquakes … the cooing of doves and the nightingale that announces the name "that I must always have in my mouth," these are my language teachers. I must indeed write this hell of cries for the paradise of narratives full of spirit to be born, in meaning.

I then heard women's voices. Suddenly, some meaning! One might have thought that by the walls of the tent villages behind which children were crying and near the wooden fences behind which the sheep were trembling, they were commanding the dogs to direct their defensive barking in the direction of the invasive jackals and wolves. The matrix females, poised in their places, were protecting the fruit of their womb and the meat and milk that fed their little ones. Language is born to protect births.

And, in fact, above the enormous score – to which, over the fluctuations of the wind and the grapeshot of the ice on the tent canvas, the howlings of the pack and the yaps of the jackals that the barking of the dogs wanted to stop were added – flew, very shrill, burst forth from these clamors and as though born from them, some cries of coloratura soprano about which you would have sworn that their meaning, emanating from the whole, well-rooted in the thickness of the sonorous score, was torn up from these clamors and, indeed, flew above. Born from these women. The eddying chaos, vociferating, gave birth to these voices; they emerged from it. Imperious, tearful, they chanted shrill cries, orders that hovered, like they say the first breaths did, upon the confusion of the primeval waters. Thus spirit was born from the noise. The wind and the wolves rose toward the women, the rumbling and the cries vibrating toward meaning. We heard the world open, express itself, clamor, rumble, call, demand, invade, fear, be moved, forbid. I'm telling the story of the world beginning to tell it's story.

THIRD MEDITATION ON OUR WAYS OF KNOWING
What did the Mediterranean seem to be saying to me when, returning from Algiers, my youth thought that

the waves of bad weather were coming along the ship to dictate to me what steps to take? What anger raised those waves, what passion? What was the Coolidge couloir chanting, when at earliest daybreak it was filling the vertical walls of ice with irradiations of mauve and pink, other than: *Deum de Deo, lumen de lumine*. It seemed to say it so powerfully, and in such good Latin, that our guide turned around to ask me what we, wicked non-believers, had heard. What were the furious waters to the south of Crete clamoring – the winter when, on Sea Ten, I entered adulthood by the front door – across the disheveled walls raised before the prow whose heading I was attempting to steer according to the storm conditions? What was the singing bass thundering that came from an unknown depth of the ground during the Loma Prieta earthquake, when everything was collapsing around me? What was the hurricane whistling at Puerto Rico, whose wind was laying the coconut trees parallel to the ground and preventing our plane from landing? With what dense silence did the Red Sea formerly welcome my ecstatic night watches? And with what fearsome whisperings and silky tearings did Garonne's inundations threaten my father's sandpits? And what did Noah hear at the door of the Bosphorus? In these inhuman encounters, the world presented itself, gave, sounded warnings and left a mute science in my soul, to which the soul's subsequently acquired knowledge closed all access. I would like to share this muffled understanding but can't since it's never transmitted along human sentences. How would my words let the world without words speak without me? Can I efface myself enough to let it ring?

Slowly, I'm progressing. I was just saying the said of things, then the said of the living: rats, jackals, wolves, dogs and women guards. I have therefore said the said of bodies. I will say that of trees. I'm struggling against language; I shout with the body. It hears, for its part, voices and noises: stomach, legs and thorax, head, eyes and ears, hair and nervous system. It sees better when it visits, the language says so; it hears better when it travels. Moves, stirs, trembles. It's made up of as many codes as things. Bodies recount the codes of the world.

My body that bleeds, shouts, suffers, is moved, sheds real tears, walks, runs, stops, shudders, sweats, encounters, laughs and blesses other bodies, inert, living, feminine, moving bodies. My body animated with vortices or whirlwinds that are sometimes in phase with the movements of the world. These movements of mine, my language calls them by the same name: emotions. I am therefore recounting my emotions when they encounter the emotions of other bodies and the emotions of the Biogea.

The wind was whistling, trembling; the ice crystals were crackling, strafing; the wolves were howling and vibrating; the jackals yapping and shivering; the baying of the guard dogs was vibrating; the women were commanding, calling, shivering; in the tent, our bodies vibrated and trembled with fear, anxiety, joy, emotions.

Everything was vibrating, the tent canvas, the wild voices and our bellies. Everything was trembling, singing, crying, praying and chanting. Everything stirs, of course, everything evolves, everything changes and moves, but by trembling, with emotion. Therefore by sending out signals, of distress, hope and joy. Therefore by inventing a language. Everything speaks. How is it we don't yet have anything said or written in this universal language?

We climbed back down, much later, from the Everest massif, safe and sound, enraptured, exhausted, happy, frozen stiff, tranquil for life, instructed in a knowledge that we were never able to share with the people of the cities made hard of hearing by the stercoraceous, technological, media and political hubbub.

HYMN TO THE TREE OF KNOWLEDGE

She in her garden, amidst the mute flora. Her absurd profession: meetings, fast food, long-winded colloquia, round tables, media, dense schedules, the day passes, night falls. Exhausted, curled up in her bed, Eve sleeps and dreams. She gets back up. Goes through the doorway. Some force, but it matters little, transports her into the park. Slow and powerful, another holds her motionless and straightens her, floral, toward the vertical. Her heels sink into the viscous humus up to her ankles; her toes grow longer and run like moles in tunnels narrower than threads; her trunk loses its flexibility and becomes wooden, knotty; her arms rise up, her fingers spin out toward the trellis that reigns at the top of the garden and where, already, her hair is tousling and sliding; then from her mouth, from her nostrils, from her genitals and apple breasts, pink flowers of springtime flow superabundantly, all entwined with the mauve clusters of an Adam come here, a gentle wisteria set in motion by the breeze. Tied, knotted, braided, the spread out serpentine garland climbing around the tree bouquet shines in the night. Nothing moves or comes to tilt the tranquil perenniality of this happy intertwining. Eve rejoices at the white magnificence of the scarlet petals emanating from her organs changed into boughs.

The sun rises. Eve wakes in her bed. She slept well. An absurd profession, a busy schedule. In a hurry, she runs; meetings, fast food, long-winded colloquia, hubbub … she passes, running, in front of the impeccable apple tree. Shock: she has just learned that she sits enthroned there. So Eve has a double? Not a twin, nor a mirror image, nor a strange fantasy like one has in depression, but an exact and mysterious correspondent in the universe of the living whose sovereign beauty teaches her how much her loves are beautiful.

Botanical garden, paradise.

HYMN TO THE OAK AND THE LINDEN
An archaic habitat for silent hamadryads, the ancient spring of my childhood and its weeping willows made way for a roaring pump and black pipes. A house of cool shadows for slow crawfish and frog jumps, the stream of my adolescence became a concrete V through which a pipe went. Tearing up the hedges, formerly and long ago aligned along my plough and oxen, to connect the fields and so that tractors could run there, next leveling the ground with a bulldozer transformed the garden of France two times over. What barbarians made a hell, unitary and flat, of my old rural Eden, composite? Where is the door through which one can return to it?

I discovered it in Creuse. I wasn't born there. I had never been there until my old years, yet I find myself back there. My memories no longer lie in the Garonne plain, but there. Here is my country, my peasants, my diverse landscapes with small plots separated by green, the ancient relation to the land and animals, in which industry, finance, banks, the market economy … have not yet imposed either their format or their law on life. Finally I'm at home. First memory, returning home.

Plus the trees. In the Landes, the Vosges, the Alps, Amazonia, the Rockies or Siberia, you can cross forests, pines or firs of shadow, monotonous birches or similar spruces; even the groves in the Vendée or Poitou show willows and poplars. Never like here.

The Creuse exhibits a paradise of isolated trees. The king oak, the beech, the hornbeam, the chestnut, the centenary linden and the colossal sequoia, the elegant cedar displaying its pagoda, sometimes the maple: each one, on its own, explodes in its essence. Spread out at leisure in its platonic heaven, it realizes its vital idea by freely, vividly, madly occupying the surrounding area as though in a strictly geometric volume: perfect balls or spheres, dilated with joy, cones rigorous with vigor, varied stories.… The Tree spreads itself out to the optimum of its type, unique, individuated, wrapped in its glorious magnificence and in the luxurious and trembling plurality of its hazards. Like a stabilized vortex of life. The Creuse welcomes the pure concept of every species into its space and places this concept, quivering, into its exact compartment. Botanical and silvicultural plates, clumsy, will copy out reality, here concrete and ideal at the same time. Paradise: the place where the real rejoins the rational; where life attains the perfection of being.

Beech, oak, linden, cedar or chestnut … achieve, here, three times, a feat that one will, yes, only see in paradise, or that was never seen except in the garden of Eden: the ecstasy of their idea; the exuberant explosion of their vital force in the vortex of the crown; the concrete perception, here and now, of the thing of the world, displayed in its beauty. Creuse: the orgasm of trees! I don't write "orgasm" fortuitously since this word signifies, since the ancient Greek doctor Hippocrates, the plenitude of sap and vigor in a living thing swollen with food and vitality; two millennia later, his successor Lamarck made use of the same word to convey the physiological tension of sensitive life. So here paradise shows itself, realized in and through the orgasm of arborescence.

Pierre Barbizet, a pianist of immense talent, had fingerings shown to him by Yves Nat, for whom we both felt admiration and respect. At his final course – he died soon after – the uncontested master of his generation opened the door for Pierre and, in dismissing him with a tranquil smile, said to him: "Become a tree!" For myself, who was dragging my clumsiness behind these geniuses of the piano, I have always remembered and tried to apply this advice for orgiastic and paradisiacal production, wide with spreading and lightness.

Second memory. For the country and the peasantry, I've returned to the nether side of the dominant global economy by, let's say, a half century. But, for the trees, I've regressed from this agricultural France to Gaul. Of course, I'm authorized by the granite, from which the Creusois masons drew so many masterpieces, including those jagged walls in *opus incertum*, as well as by the ancient menhirs and dolmens, plus the quays of Lyon, the streets of Paris and the Bordelaise marvels, but these stones, inert, only address my head, I mean the memories of history, the one you learn in school that lies so often. Inert stones.

Whereas the wood of these trees speaks to the muscles of my trunk, their bark to my skin, their sap to my blood; yes, I feel their boughs rise up like my members. I have a hard-on like a branch. Here, Adam metamorphoses into an oak and Eve into a linden, as it is told of Philemon, who loved Baucis so much that on the eve of their deaths Hermes and Jupiter changed them both into each of these two trees. And when the wind blew, the one would still caress tenderly, with his branches, the splendid twigs of the other, spread out in her feminine beauty.

If I stay here three weeks, I become the peasant of my childhood again, level with the diversified hedges, vanished back home; but if I were to remain here ten years, I'd be afraid of becoming a druid or the priest with the golden bough. I'd climb up the branches of the trees to pick the ritual mistletoe with

124

a yellow sickle. I no longer know then whether I'd be changed into the priest who cuts either into the oak itself or into the cut epiphyte. No: I wouldn't forget that I became an oak so as to enter once again into my beautiful linden.

At a crossroads of sunken lanes, between Peyrat-la-Nonière and La Fressenède, but it must be said in twenty similar spots, the recent converts to Christianity erected a cross on a pedestal, like a Breton calvary. In this place, below that altar, an ancient temple was concealed, for the dark grove is sleeping in the shade of the oaks' grandiose perfection. Reasonable barbarians, instinctively the Moderns didn't touch it. Sure of its antiquity, my entire body trembles with memory and fright when I approach this sacred wood. It is the same age as me tree.

The metamorphosis of anamnesis has begun. How would I know whether my flesh, transformed into this woody trunk, is climbing with its foliage toward the light or descending into the earth by following its roots? Beloved of Adam-Philemon-oak, Eve-Baucis-linden accompanied him, the way Beatrice guided Dante either to Hell, below the dark soil, or to Seventh Heaven, in the air of the bright canopies. Profound and happy, they are both following the doubly vertical path of trees.

But I'm staying here for too little time. Behold: I'm finally residing there with the entire life of oak me and the entire life of linden her. So a third memory besieges me when another metamorphosis arises. At the moment when, dressed in such a way that I can only laugh at it, the druid, armed with that laughable sickle, is devoting himself to the ridiculous rite of the mistletoe, I – who, *I*, the Gascon or the Creusois, the Frenchman or the Gaul, the peasant or the scientist, the rationalist or the one in love who is writing this narrative, me the priest or the two trees? – I therefore ask myself what the deep cause of such an ascent is.

Where is the druid – or the priest with the golden bough – heading when he slowly climbs into the crown's vortex? What, in so doing, does he remember? I think he's returning to that place I've been seeking to go back to myself ever since my narrative, begun today, has been leading me. From Gascony to Creuse, yes; from Paris to my childhood, yes again; from urban politics to the rural world; from today's France to forgotten Gaul; from the wayside cross to the sacred wood; from my rational science to the primitive druidism about which no one knows anything; from my body to the tree trunk, why not? I am there, at the same time as that ancestor making a gesture about which I don't know anything.

Both climb into the tree together. Into this oak I have become, into the linden you are becoming, aided by the memory and the metamorphosis of bodies. And here comes a third memory charging down in waves upon us, in a wave of blindly corporal memories, an incredible anamnesis that brings us back to the nether side of Lucy, to the age without any clear memory, when we – Hominidae, Homininae, quasi-chimpanzees – were still living among the branches, our old habitat, our primitive house.

Here I am finally back home. Not only into the Creuse, not only into the countryside, into the time and space of my rural childhood – fifty years – not only into ancient Gaul, amid the granite and the mistletoe of the ritual festivals – two thousand years – not only into the branches of your arms, but into those of the tree that you, you have become, that I have become, into the princely path of light towards earth and from the soil to the heights, to the primordial house from which we are, both of us – millions and millions of years ago – descended, before our kneecaps locked up, even before we could walk, upright, in the wooded savannah.

Wooded like the Creuse.

Us, upright, risen, vertical for the first time, trees among trees, chin and neck straightened up, springing from the hell soil to the heaven sky, displaying a new confidence and a new pride.

Displaying among the wooded.

Fourth Meditation on our Ways of Knowing

When at their deaths, they became oak and linden, in what language did Eve-Baucis and Adam-Philemon confess their affection while caressing their boughs? Are there "dendron" dialects? Can I understand them?

Not only do I not speak Korean or Quechua, but my father made fun of my mother because the Gascons didn't pronounce *pain* [bread] with the intonation of the Quercynois. We've quadrangled the Earth with human languages that are opaque to one another. Hatred or biodiversity? Happily, we're doing better: Facebook sends my granddaughter's photo, located in Paris, to the far reaches of Cape Horn and Kamchatka. Will some Inuit, or a Fuegean, another inhabitant of the New Hebrides be fascinated by her profile? But also: an earthquake along the coastline of Chile causes, not many hours later, a devastating tsunami on the shores of Japan. El Niño spreads ocean and atmospheric currents, brush fires, thunderstorms and droughts around the world.

Who communicates the best, the fastest, the farthest, the strongest? Us, by the Internet, or these elements of the world: fire, earth and water? Some patch or other of Sun occasions, at its surface, a rise in its temperature whose gradient produces, at some latitude or other of the globe, a hurricane that drives high waves onto some beach or other and brings torrential rain to some forest or other, whose mangroves, at its edge, are going to grow so much that the surrounding avian fauna, profiting from the canopies, will proliferate during that season and will multiply the distribution, in that area, of seeds whose flowers the bees, come the season, will contribute to pollinating, thereby creating a source of delicious honey, that some tribe or another.... I can recount a thousand chains of this type, which show that the world, connected like our networks, was becoming globalized from its foundation; and that we are imitating this process.

Caused, causing, all things in the world ensue from each other, chained together. Whether fluid or of air – even solids communicate – things respire together, they conspire with different breaths, but in a constant and total circulation that's chancy, torn, chaotic and consenting. These breaths have rhythms, *tempi*, a music, waves, codes. Caused, causing, certainly, but coding, coded, I say again. The world adds up the codes. Let's change the word *chose* [thing]; formerly and long ago, it copied out the term *cause*. *Causa*, in Latin; *cosa*, in Italian; *chose* lastly, in French. Now, at least as much as causing-caused through force or power, attraction and repulsion, impact and accretion ... things, coded, code other things, just as coded as they are and, thus, become coding together. Let's forget causes for the moment in favor of codes;

the old root, hard, mechanical, in favor of the new one, soft, computing.

Just as we've broken the transparent mirror of language into pieces so that not only the Koreans and the Inuit but even the Quercynois don't understand the Gascons, we've likewise split up the knowledge of the world and divided science into languages that are quite opaque to one another: astronomy for the sky, physics and chemistry on earth, biology for flora and fauna, sociology for humans, etc. One philosopher has even spoken of the conflict of the faculties to describe the rivalries between fields of knowledge, rivalries analogous to wars between nations or to enemy brothers. Taking continual pleasure from confirming the truth of the perennial work of Empedocles's hate, we practice, venerate, recommend, and privilege the analysis that divides while believing the debate that contradicts will somehow transform into a dynamic momentum.

Knowledge is changing today. The all-political is dying; the monarchy of the sciences said to be hard is coming to a close. The science of the things of the world will have to communicate just as much as the things of the world do, which do it much better than humans do, who don't always want to do it. Let's celebrate two changes this morning. The first one strikes a new blow to our narcissism. No, knowledge and the world don't resemble our analytical enjoyments of refined cutting up, of endless debates and of exclusions full of hate. They, on the contrary, form a bloc and a sum, alliance and alloys.

Uniting the fields of knowledge among themselves the way the things are connected among themselves, the second newness puts into place sets united by interlacings, webs and simplexes that combine with the things of the world, themselves combined, the combined knowledge that understands them.

I think I hear that these interfering networks, crisscrossed like ten stringed, wind and percussion instruments from an orchestra, resonating like the echoes of codes. Coded-coding, each thing reverberates in every other thing, coding-coded. I also hear the fuzzy set of these reverberations.

So, these things – formerly mute and said to be objective because passive like the slaves of an activity that would belong only to us – these coding-coded things, as though awakened, speak just as much and perhaps better than us, they also say, write, sing, communicate among themselves, through a kind of reciprocal encoding, a kind of common language, a kind of music, harmonic, disharmonic – I don't know yet – but whose voices I am sure to hear. Solo, duo, trio, quartet … and *tutti*, in sum.

Therefore when, due to a gust of wind, the boughs of the oak caress the crown of the linden in great numbers, do I really hear Philemon confess his love to

Baucis and her welcome it: annunciation, visitation, assent? No, not at all, I no longer need, like Ovid or La Fontaine long ago, these two figures to obtain a human translation of it. By erasing these theater masks and these capricious divinities, I truly hear the oak itself conversing with the linden. They exchange, certainly, titmice and nightingales, mockingjays, chaffinches and sparrows, their feathers, their songs, their trills; but, in addition, a thousand secret codes that we don't yet know how to analyze. The two old people die a second time. Better, I have even less need, to express what I mean, for tropes, as readers sometimes say, who, putting their fingers in their ears, expel the truth of the world and its beauty into poetry, poorly viewed today, a truth and beauty that they themselves no longer see.

No, I simply take pleasure in the obviousness of understanding in truth, since it remains true that beyond the two trees moaning beneath the gust of the zephyr or of a breath of desire, all things, coded, store and process information, and, coding, receive it from others and transmit it to others. With an entirely rational ear, I intercept – in dendron language! – the oak-linden dialogue. Like, just now, the invasions, reciprocal and howling, of the rats, wolves, jackals, dogs, and the shouts the women, guardians of lambs and children.

I understand why we formerly described an unstable, therefore trustworthy, dinghy as *jaloux* [jealous]. It hugs the chop marvelously; with a meticulous and immediate exactitude, it details each little breeze of wind. The sea announces itself through waves and, a perfect sailor, the dory's form allows it to respond. There's no little wave that doesn't provoke a little roll in it. I have sailed in the love dialogue – held there in nautical language – of a dory and a stormy bay, off Newfoundland.

Likewise, every fragile breeze induces this oak branch to provoke a response from that linden twig, trembling and adapted to it. They listen to each other like no human couple ever spoke to one another. Yes, the sciences are beginning to discover it, the trees themselves emit voices.

Who chatters in concert? The things of the world. Who speaks in total? The Biogea itself. I wager that, tomorrow, advanced science will attempt to reproduce these orchestrations of Flora and Fauna and publish the scores.

Encounters, Loves

An old Brest tradition has the Navy, on summer Sundays, moor a ship said to be for visiting on the banks of the Penfeld below the pont de Recouvrance. For several hours, the ship was opened to the greedy curiosity of tourists. Free entry, intimidated crowd, impatient line, children around one's legs. To the joy of the sailors, the guests confused port and starboard, stern and bow, became distressed in the alleyways, got their feet tangled in the ranges of cables lying about the deck, swallowed hook, line and sinker the perfidious blarney told by the quartermasters, who, as guides, mouthed stern frame, boom, spun-yarn and sheer in front of the landsmen, mouths agape. Disguised as instructors from another world, we had fits of mad laughter in recounting just about anything: that we'd arrived that very morning from Cape Horn – a large swell, ma'am, cries of petrels amid the ice floe, low and black clouds, shipwrecks, sir, alas many people shipwrecked. Oh no, spending vacation Sundays having people visit the ship wasn't a chore.

That day, we'd arrived, in fact, from high latitudes, on a mission of assistance to the Newfoundland fishermen: a little surgery, pharmaceutical products, pumping of fuel, mail, mechanical repairs, a little human warmth in these misty waters strewn with drifting icebergs. Admiring the proliferating richness of the banks beneath the enormous population of fishermen, we didn't yet suspect, neither the fishermen nor us, the extent of the devastation. Years later, having returned to St. John's for other reasons, I learned from despairing experts that the cod – the local fortune and tasty delight when eaten fresh – would probably never come back. Like many other species, these large fish, voracious and naïve, live in tight colonies in order to be able to reproduce: the female and the male wouldn't be able to encounter each other in the three dimensional aquatic space, immense, without first grouping themselves in dense assemblies. Should excessive fishing make them scarce, the sexes losing their way, the encounter would no longer take place. We have so much difficulty, we pedestrians of two flat dimensions, in finding one another that we can imagine our anxieties if, distraught, vertiginous along the vertical, we swam or flew into the excess. No more love, no more joy; no more newness, no more learning. No more encounters.

I've forgotten the date. On duty, I was on watch while we were docked; night was falling. The last visitor had just crossed the gangplank. The skipper hailed me over the loudspeaker. I ran to his cabins. "Midshipman," he said to me, "go down to the gangway. You'll find an old bore there who claims to be holding enough official papers to look, straight in the eyes, at our innermost organs, I mean those that, normally, we classify as 'top secret.' Verify his statements, and depending, expel him without hesitation or guide him at leisure. I have neither the time nor the desire to please this bore."

Rushing to the guardroom, who did I see? Tournesol in person, yes, the scientist Tryphon, small, agile, goateed, big head, high forehead, but without glasses, seeming in the pleasant clouds, in discussion with the boatswain, as infinitely courteous with him as if he were addressing Castafiore herself. The boatswain held the documents out to me, signed by various ministers with portfolio and starred admirals, most certainly authentic. Smiling, I put myself at the disposal of our guest.

We went all over the ship, quite deserted at that hour, a part of the crew having disembarked to finish their Sunday on land. Visibly, nothing interested him, not the bridge, nor navigation, nor the weapons; head in the air, he seemed to look only at the radar basket. We descended to the electrical equipment, to the ASDICs. Here he was finally attentive. Asked a first question, which I answered; a second, I knew; a third, yes again; a fourth, good; at the fifth, I got a little muddled; at the following one, I stammered; I admitted myself to be, in the final analysis, out of my depth. Mute as a mackerel. "Do forgive me, sir, I haven't completely mastered the highest mysteries of quantum mechanics." He watched me splutter with the gentle amiability of the high-level expert who understands and pardons the ignorance of those who trouble about the subject of particles. He caressed the apparatus with his left hand, ungloved. "Were you here, young man, when it was brought aboard?" "Yes, sir." "Have you checked its functioning?" "Several times and it works perfectly." "I'm delighted; I came to make sure." "Oh?" I said surprised. "Yes, I invented the principle of it several years ago; it took some time for me to perfect it; I gladly visit the prototypes that are in place to check their effectiveness." And he launched, and launched me with him, into a crystal clear explanation, whose memory I have kept intact, so much did the world into which he was inviting me to enter seem to be fascinating and new. Up till then I had been playing the role of guide, I became the visitor filled with wonder.

While he was lavishly unwinding his demonstration, an anxiety was choking me by the throat and must have shown through despite my polite and so quickly charmed appearance. For neither I nor the skipper had cared to read the identity of this additional evening visitor on the papers, and I was ashamed, then, to ask him right out of the blue: so who are you, to have gone so deep into the atom and the electron? He had the tactful intuition to see that question pass behind my distraught eyes. He simply told me his name. I nearly fell to the ground.

I gave my report to the skipper; by the time he understood his blunder, the apparition had vanished.

I will never forget that encounter, which I still live like a blessing. For I had the unmerited good fortune that this great man, esteemed everywhere for his wit and humility, would later invite me over to his home and befriend me. During the summer, Francis Perrin lived on the Côtes-d'Armor in the famous place that the people named Sorbonne-Plage and which was the sparkling center of knowledge during the twentieth century. He taught me more and better than science: the entry into a new world. In welcoming me like a member of his family, he opened the gates of a palace for me whose splendor I would never have suspected and that, a young midshipman, I swore I'd never leave.

But I already knew where to enter paradise. When I wasn't yet twelve years old, I knew, by heart and by body, Garonne and my dredger, the plowshares of the plow and the oxen under the yoke, the declensions and mass in Latin: rough and ready. As the learned would have said formerly: natural, not cultural.

Taking refuge in our Aquitainian region because of the war, a friend from class was born, for his part, in South America, of a Chilean mother who had married a Frenchman, a talented engineer, a manager of several copper and silver mines at the foot of the Andes. A whole other world. She played Chopin and Ravel marvelously. On behalf of his parents, my friend one day invited me to accompany him to the concert; he held out a ticket to me. A concert? What was it about? I followed him reluctantly, so much would I have preferred going to the stadium to applaud, with my brother, my favorite team, rugby champions.

Our seats were next to the stage. The lights went out. A woman in a long dress came forward, bowed and took a seat before the piano. Suddenly, a shower of gems rained over my savage and ill-combed head, a dense cascade of gems, black diamonds, scarlet rubies, blue velour emeralds, sapphires encrusted around a fountain from which gushed the drink of immortality, prepared, that evening, by this musician, come from Paris expressly to tear off my old skin. Elegant, slipping behind the basin of dream, she opened a porch which I then crossed for the first time. No more war, no more sorrow, no more hatred, no more lowland, no more sweat or floods, no more breakdowns, no more cables that break, no more tears, except for those, new, unforeseeable, caused to stream by joy. Cataracts. And if pain remained, a magic ingredient made it shine, incandescent, and transparent, burn. I suspected that it was about beauty. I swore then never to leave the world I had just entered, carried by this Prelude written by Frédéric Chopin and caressed by Jeanne-Marie Darré. Who I have never, since, seen or heard.

She taught me the door of paradise. Since, I have known that Beatrice exists, the guide, the accompanist who conducted Dante into the improbable, vertiginous spaces of reality.

Here we have a second doorway. Under the shadow of the porch that opened onto the street, one couldn't see anything or anybody; not a sound was to be heard. Nothing. Nothing was happening. Silence. He, guided, was leaving, discreet; guide, she accompanied him to the door. Polite, he hardly touched her; courteous, she hardly defended herself. A gentle caress happened, like a feather gliding in the silky air. Nothing noteworthy took place.

At the same time, millions of light-years away, strange myriads of characters with transparent bodies, equipped, for a number of them, with forty pairs of wings awoken from the virtual somnolence into which eternity had plunged them by an immediate commotion; enthusiasts of the minuscule event, inspired by its softness, they quickly grabbed hold of musical instruments – organs, trombones, gongs, oboes and accordions, trumpets, violins and clarinets, tambourines and castanets – so as to launch, at once, into a triumphal fanfare, while countless choirs sang with twenty declaiming voices the ringing praises of this terrestrial nothing that, in the shadow of the porch, hardly took place. In an instant comparable to the big bang, the entire universe expanded with the music of their brass and the ringing of their tubas.

Just before playing, singing, the composing angels, the executing cherubim, the virtuoso thrones had heard the silky feather caress illuminating the dark porch with its warmth. Simultaneously, caresser and caressed heard ringing timpani, thundering organs and chiming church bells millions of light-years from there. For a hyperaesthesic hearing, a seventh sense unknown to the others but common to those in love and archangels, short-circuits the rare silences of this vulgarly noisy and cruelly hard world with the triumphal fanfares of the seventh heaven. The ones whispered lower, the others rang higher. Only then does our globe, dull and terraqueous, communicate with the paradise lost, attain its fire and light. Without this sense, as much aerial as feather and silk, there would be no love, no song or beatitude.

Here is the score sung by the celestial choirs accompanied by this orchestra: overflowing with insolent theology, it declaims that the angels wouldn't exist, that they would have remained plunged within the eternal virtual, with no chance of ever being born into divine light, if no caress had ever passed, light, over the happy skin of the girls of the Earth. The caress alone revives them from the apathetic sleep of the spheres … *l'amor che muove il sole e l'altre stelle.*

A minor variant on the same score simply changes sign to powers of ten in the calculation of the distance between the ringing of the tubas and the shadowed porch: not an immense distance in millions of light-years, but a tight proximity in billionths of angstrom. For the triumphal fanfare rings less in the back-worlds than under the arch of the womb, in the intimacy of the uterus, at the point of silence where the word, scarcely conceived, shudders with joy for the first time.

Conversely, I also descended to the Underworld. Everyone has had to enter, the way I did then, into the holy of holies that the clinics and hospitals devote to intensive care, often situated in the antechamber of the end. As much for the germs as for the mourning, they dress you there, from head to foot, in a preliminary airlock, in virgin white or bottle green, and thus caparisoned, shod, coiffed, wrapped, you are permitted to have a conversation for a few minutes with him or her whose survival the medical profession, with science and solicitude, hopes for.

On a beautiful October afternoon, at the Tondu Clinic in Bordeaux, I saw, not death, but love, like I see the sky from here; yes, I have seen death, the foul-smelling whore of these places, submit to silent love. You would have thought him scarcely thirty-five years old, with his Greek shepherd's hair, his curly blond chin beard, his eyes so blue they seemed white, his faded navy shoes the ends of which were peeking out from under his blue twill pants – for, against every sensible precept, he was lying fully stretched out amid the wires and rubber tubes – but you would have above all seen, short and callused from hoisting the halyards and lowering in the cables, his hands, which he was running, gently caressing, over the most hideously wrinkled face and body I had ever seen under Satan's sun. She was dying from one cancer and ten cures, whose metastases and radiations had devoured skin and muscles, nerves and other organs, relations and gaze, color and light, until nothing was left but a small pile of gray bones. What did it matter, he was showing love, still and always. Was he making dawnings of energy rain down on her so as to aid her in her final dying hours? Was he breathing the wind of his strength into her to keep her alive? In any case, he was working the way God no doubt did before his Sunday, when the elements and living creatures were barely appearing in the light. He was fighting, human, against the base world. And she was existing. These two athletes of life taught me that the Lord, during his creative week, had combated death with his breath and living strength so as to introduce into the world a rebirth. I saw, in this unified double body, although forever defeated, the invisible action of the love that, at every moment, lifts my weakness with its breath.

Seen from this deep hell, I have since known how things are with triumph.

Whose lowest doors sometimes conceal treasures. Everyone in town knew Maurice, the fiddler. He would regularly walk around it in the morning, between nine and eleven, and stand in the lanes and courtyards playing *La Vie en rose* and *Le Temps des cerises* beneath the windows. Bareheaded, the housewives would throw him coins from the windows. Who lent an ear to the intense delicacy of his vibrato? He lived alone, out of the way, on Garonne's right bank between the watercress beds, among the nettles and the reeds, in a battered trailer out of which the smoke from his cooking would come in the evening.

One morning, brought to his doorstep by an aimless walk, I heard, behind the rickety door of his shack, the grand Ciaconna. Motionless for a good while, I thought I recognized a recording by Yehudi Menuhin. Maurice appeared at the hole that served as his window, made a sign to me, opened the protective cover of his box and descended the three planks of the stepladder that was balancing between the wheels. Old, stooped, wrapped in a gray sweater fringed at the cuffs that was too large for his thin frame, he told me, in a cracking voice, that he had noticed my appreciation of his playing, that he was in pain, that he was going to die, that he would like … he stammered. This loner made little use of words. He brandished his instrument:

"Can you do me a service … keep a secret for me? You know … I'm playing *Le Président* … I no longer have the ability, of course."

He hesitated, fearful; finally began:

"Don't think, this Stradivarius, I didn't steal it; I won it long ago … oh, so long ago. The whole rest of my life, I've made the trailer its case and hiding place… there, better than my body. When I die, come by and take it from on my bed, right next to my immobility, bring it to … also give her the new scores that I composed for her these last years … as for the name of she who didn't want me, I will imprint it on my soul."

This other world of knowledge, beauty, love or despair, I will only enter this true world, more real than real, guided by the happenstance of my wanderings in the wide open, between the mad laughs or the more frequent mad tears. No one enters without a guide who indicates and incarnates it, without crossing a gangway, an airlock, a bridge, an interchange, without a porter who opens the door, an angel who announces it, without a custom's tollgate. Without an encounter.

When traveling for a long time, you suddenly discover the Devil or God, either one or the other or both. Everything happens while traveling: from the skipper's cabins to Sorbonne-Plage; from the dredger gathering up rocks to the pianist whose hands poured out corundum and beryl, in cataracts; from a dark doorstep to the seventh heaven or the subcircles of hell. But also: from Troy to Ithaca on a boat, for Ulysses, wandering on the verses of the *Odyssey*; stop: seven years of happiness with Calypso. From Jerusalem to forty furlongs further, for the pilgrims of Emmaus; stop: the Lord himself, eating a meal. Tobias traveled on foot with nothing less than an archangel and Jacques, on horse behind his master…. Let's be on our way! One can also travel quite simply in time, from childhood to old age, for the journey takes place across ordinary space or in life; or across age or through ten landscapes, transports in any case. And then.…

Where were we, my child, in the story I was telling you next to your bed before you feel asleep last night? And the child of man answers: "We were at: *and then*." A storyteller only knows these two words. I walk here, elsewhere, it doesn't matter, and then the encounter happens. It changes the world. Rebirth.

Ulysses sailed, and then came across sirens, sorceresses, cyclopses, thunderstorms, becalming, shipwreck. Tobias walked along, and then discovered Raphael, bird droppings sealed up his eyes, so he was blind; the gall of a fish healed him; his betrothed was awaiting him, the way Penelope in Ithaca hoped for a sailor who always had a facing wind. The Samaritan came down from his horse, and then found an injured man in the ditch. Jacques's new mount only knew how to climb the slope to the gallows; she only loved the hanged, what an affair! Beneath the lashing shower, Brassens offered a place to a girl under his heavenly umbrella; she had to leave it.… Hell.

I'm maintaining the hobby of prepositions. I love them; I even dream of only speaking of them, with them, by them. I write for, I live with, I go through. I collect words made up of them for the sheer pleasure of it. Over the long excursion of my language, I encounter a word: encounter. En-counter.

There are no living narratives except for flowing transports broken up, then, by these sudden impacts. You fall against. No, we never leave for, toward, to a destination, with an eye to a project or an end, for that cause said to be final loses its importance as the journey goes along; the goal is lost along the way. Circumstances: during, depending on, according to, between and toward, without, except and in return for, I almost forgot concerning. Confession: one of Ulysses's companions, I couldn't care less about almost every heading I've ever followed – don't tell me that my skipper was sailing to Ithaca. But my life and his awoke to encounters: lively, better, vital through mutations. Our paths went toward them so as to be reborn.

I'm mistaken. The route itself isn't always a matter of indifference. A few years ago, I was dining in Kyoto with a Japanese government dignitary accompanied by his wife. The conversation at our meeting quickly became lively. I was surprised: "How did you come by such precise and refined French?" "We don't deserve the credit; we lived in Paris for many years." I had the impudent tactlessness to inquire about when. "Oh! My husband," answered the wife, "was appointed ambassador to France in 1936; that forced us to remain in your capital until the end of the Second World War." More and more ill at ease, I then asked how they had been able to return to their country during the stormy overthrows of 1944-45.

"And then, we went back home on foot," they said, smiling and discreet. Dumbfounded, I cried out: "From Paris to Tokyo?" "That journey wasn't easy," they replied at the same time, "for we were crossing, at the outset as at our arrival, countries that weren't very favorably disposed to our nation; we hid ourselves during the day and made our way at night. It was difficult to sleep and to feed ourselves, even in small amounts. It took us at least two years to finally reach the Chinese shore facing our archipelago. What a pleasure then to take the boat!"

I swear to never pride myself on walking again. They didn't have the time to tell me how, conversely, they avoided all encounter.

Rare, these moments of being on the lam. Most often, everything is decided at the crossroads. The newness of the short story recognizes or fails to recognize an encounter, where quite precisely my prepositions shoot up, spurt out, swarm, exult…. I have caught a glimpse of an encounter between two doors, on the porch; after Charybdis, the sailor risks being engulfed in the maelstrom of Scylla: Oedipus kills his father at the crossroads, on a narrow bridge I think; the Samaritan stops beside the injured man: you see two close relations there, two fellow men, two victims, the beaten injured man and the excluded man from Samaria; on Circe's island, a hundred sailors disguised as pigs leave the Sorceress's salon snorting.… We recount during, before, after, for and against, encounter.… Contingency: two persons, two things, two events touch one another. Without this impact, no short story.

They were both going to Emmaus, a village on the sixtieth furlong from Jerusalem. And they were conversing about what had just happened. While they were talking, Jesus, risen, appeared, drew near and traveled with them. But their eyes were prevented from recognizing him.

Just as they were about to part ways, for the two had arrived home, they said to the stranger: "Stay with us, for night is falling." While having dinner, when he broke the bread, they recognized him … but then he vanished. I never saw Jeanne-Marie Darré again. Nor my sailor of loving unto death.

Have we ever recounted, related any other narrative than this matrixial short story? Do we live another time than this? While walking along, we don't see who is going by. We nevertheless encounter God and the Devil. The two of them hold out a hand to us. Either both or sometimes God all alone. At Emmaus, God himself, in person.

Then he vanished, like the physicist with the skipper's eyes. I had to leave her, after I said a big thank you. God went back into the dark glory of absence, and I returned to the poverty of the road, exposed to the ordinary.

When I was young, I thought you had to cross a river by swimming; that there was a goal, the opposite bank. We were all going there; we were aiming at it; we were even racing. "There it is," some said, "just a few more strokes!" Who will get there first? We even thought we could already touch bottom. Then, after years, we noticed that the current carried us beyond the estuary; no more opposite bank, ocean immensity in front; everyone lost on the open sea. We'll touch bottom no more. Only one question: winded, exhausted to the point where the heart gives out, in whose company will you swim? Alone?

The goal vanishes. Success fades. Destination? No. Everything stops here, where the silence begins. Here, at the foot of the fiddler's trailer; here, two steps from the gangway; here or in front of the bed where the sailor's fiancée is dying. A strange presence descends there. As though life, before and after, was making its way, in its entirety, to and for nothing but, here suspended, was crossing that moment of dense intensity in which the angels sing. Born for now, I was traveling toward here, stopped before that stranger who smiled at my ignorance in quantum mechanics; at the feet of that unknown woman who threw a rain of rubies with emeralds over my head. Temporary destination and address: him, now; her, then. I said to them: would you paddle, a moment, in company with me? While chatting together, we forget that we're swimming, that we're paddling about and can't touch bottom, that we're perhaps going to drown. The sailor love was caressing his small boat in distress; and his small boat was still carrying him. On the porch I should have exclaimed: stay with me, for night is falling.

Return, now, to the world. For all this, so evident in our existences, empty with goal, quickly become without goal, but whose impacts and encounters we truly live at unexpected crossroads, these births, I say, these rebirths, take place and time as much for the Biogea as in our lives, and they even took place and time well before this happens to us. That long route interrupted by splendid impacts doesn't only concern humans, but everything in the world.

And then, the narrative resumes, right at the beginning. Let's be on our way. The world explodes, begins, expands; I can recount its Grand Narrative from the beginning, at the big bang, to its end – predictable? – called the big crunch. How boring, this dull duration, unfolding in billions of years. Where is it going? Who knows? Like the narrative and I, toward Newfoundland or L'Arcouest? By what yacht? There is nothing or almost nothing to recount.

And then, along that course, perhaps senseless, how many gigantic unpredictable details, traversing this interminable time, appeared there via a thousand possible abruptnesses, emerging from it, setting about existing, being reborn, via encounters, precisely, via the impacts of galaxies, the accretions of flying dust or of asteroids forming gaseous planets, or other harder ones but equipped with scarves of atmosphere floating on their robes of sea, via black holes, gamma-ray bursts, matter gone absent, in short, a list of several thousand diverse singularities, unique, kaleidoscopic, shooting out from the nothing, strange, contingent singularities. As unpredictable as encounters with a concealed genius, a great artist or a Japanese dignitary. I can recite some of those encounters that recreate all things, perhaps I will even take centuries to tell them in simple sentences or difficult equations, theories and laws. What short stories! Nothing but smoking successes, to take your breath away. Yes, smoking, the heat that shoots out from volcanoes comes from the primeval impacts of the pieces of rocks that, banging into each other, formed the planet. In total, nothing or almost in prediction, long and empty like the ship of our lives. Everything, on the contrary, in the unpredictable, via contingent lightning bolts and impacts. Everything via the diagonal, the oblique, the inclined, the random without reason. Everything at the crossroads. Encounters.

Midshipman, descend to the gangway. Contingency: two atoms, two things, two persons touch each other. Two molecules in the Universe or in a pot mix, two particles incline their fall toward each other. Accidental crossroads: Oedipus crashed into his father on a bridge, where the son, they say, killed the father, the opposite of wars.

We don't really care whether they came from St. John's in a boat or to Bordeaux by the train, the essential thing is that amorous caress, in silence, in the shadow of death; we don't really care about the absurd, deadly, forgotten war, the essential thing is the smile above the lace tablecloth and the confession of the long journey to the Japanese archipelago; we don't really care about the quay, the essential thing is the goateed physicist, so similar to Tournesol; and even whether the Universe is running toward the crushing of the big crunch, the important thing is my planet, archaically accreted, where my umbrella opens this morning, under which Beatrice, guide, leads Dante of the old *Comedy* from hell to paradise; we really don't care that he's sailing toward Ithaca, but we're fascinated that he recounts, during a banquet at the home of a king of comedy, the cyclopses and enchantresses or that, trussed up at the base of the foremast, he lets the song of the sirens be heard by our ears; we don't care that they're walking to Emmaus, didn't they encounter the Lord on the road only to, so quickly, forget him afterward? Stay with us, for night is falling. God is incarnate there, concealed at the gangway, before the piano, on the dark porch, in the intensive care unit. I don't care about my death. Since I encountered her between two doors, on the porch. That one, I don't know how or why, clumsy, I failed to seduce her; I should have told her my life story.

Perhaps she knew it better than me, life. She could therefore have said that it began here, on said accreted planet, around the year minus four billion, and contingently. That, shy, it replicated itself, doubled itself, reproduced itself; nothing could be more boring than that repeated scissiparity that only seeks its selfish stubbornness; there's nothing to say about that restarted recopying, but then relaunched, through encounters, in Flora and Pomona, then in strange tiny creatures for so long … for a perpetual outpouring of unpredictable newness.

Encounters again, as though in vortices: microbes, bacteria, red, green algae, bright beneath the hydrogenated sun, a thousand kinds of dark mushrooms, enormous ferns, giant reptiles, dinosaurs for horror films, trap-door spiders, baobabs, elephants, praying mantises, scorpions, and under the tall and dark green cedars two intelligent fox cubs, all and always different … not to mention the grass of the fields and naked Venus coming out of the seas. Every species diverse, every individual singular, indeed unique. Nothing but mutants. Like us, the world never ceases to discover or form other worlds, evolution of the living across successive geological periods.

We don't care about the dull journey or the selfish gene that only wants to restart, but how many singularities traversed by life remain to be recounted? How many master-strokes to take your breath away, one more unexpected than the other? How much unrestrained inventiveness, continual newness, how many branches, stems, spiral or fan shells, languages, tentacles, feet, lianas, leaves, flowers and hearts, not to mention the genitalia that perpetually strive as well towards the encounter, seduction, to the feathers of every color displayed in the bird court of love, to their songs of springtime for attracting females, to the fertilisine expanded to trap the males, but also, and at the very end, to the narratives that I'm recounting poorly to make my lady friend laugh?

Yes, I've learned that love codes and mutates, for everyone as well as for us. I don't know much, on the other hand, about biochemistry, which speaks learnedly about it. So I love saying it in my way. Here it is.

In the English language, snobbery speaks Latin since, formerly, in the registration lists of the posh universities, at Oxford or Cambridge, the sons of the *nouveau riche* bourgeois, not being able to put forward any title of barony or marquisate, were formerly forced to write, in the *ad hoc* column opposite their

157

names: *s(ine) nob(ilitate)*, without nobility, from which was derived, as we know, the pseudo-English but pure fruit of Latin: snob. Considered unworthy in company of the well-born, they overdid it with the ribbons, carnations, perfumes, trinkets or handlebar mustaches.

Later our snobbery, reversed, became focused on the English language, an unexpected thing for a country in which during the Middle Ages a mathematician of genius, ashamed to call himself Hollywood, had himself called Sacrobosco. Formerly in France, the nobles spoke French, while their peasants, my ancestors and forefathers, chattered the diverse patois: Gascon, Picard or Breton. Today the dominant – like we say for dogs – massacre the various Englishes: the dialects of the Stock Exchange or management, the business schools ... leaving the French language for the use of the poor. After having spoken patois, I write once again in the dialect of a commoner.

Thus, Mr. and Mrs. S. pepper their speech with locutions and terms that showed they often took the *jet* to the west. Wealthy, they recently had a twenty-room country house built in Provence, a pleasant place to spend their slack time when they weren't sailing aboard their yacht in the quay. The shell finished, they decided to name their little love nest LOVE. Passing through Manhattan, they discovered, amused, a kitschy glass jewelry and ironmongery shop where they bought the four letters of this word, forged by hammer and of an exquisitely bad taste. They sent them by registered mail in a jumble to the mason in charge of the finishing work and at their return had the surprise of seeing, displayed in glory above the door: VELO.

Mutations create newness by making errors in the copying out of a code.

Better still: in my earliest youth, I lived this type of abortive coding. Poor, I didn't have enough money to buy shoes and would drag two shabby clod-hoppers about below my pants. One summer evening, a happy misfortune made me eligible for a competitive examination for excellence. The oral examination had to be taken before a jury of examiners with hats, canes and ties. One had to dress up for it. I used up my credit on a pair of patent leather shoes that caused me awful pain. Walking in them was impossible. I hid these shiny objects in my schoolbag and, in sight of Olympus, changed in secret. At my entry into the holy of holies, one of the examiners, a famous scholar, exclaimed, rolling his *r*'s: "Documents a*rr*e fo*rrr*bidden du*rr*ing the tests!" and seized my bag. I then took the oral exam which seemed to last more than a month, with one of my judges on the altar above me lounging, arms crossed, nonchalant, on the bag of shoes. Thinking he was taking away my scholarly pomp [*pompes*], he was leaning on my worn shoes [*pompes*]. The word's double meaning, in slang, amusingly accompanied the interrogations that I underwent while laughing to seventh heaven. Never did a jury see a candidate so cheerful.

Thus mutant changes of code create new singularities. Galaxies or planets, so many wells from which to draw entertaining short stories: encounters, accretion, exchanges, errors, bifurcations. Species with Linnaean Latin names, these are the same well, another perennial source for short stories: encounters, sex and selected mutations. Again newborns, again outpouring, encounter, surprising originalities through transcription errors. Short stories: encounters of people, encounters of atoms, stars, species, living things, encounters of letters, mutations, failures of coding. Thus, commonplace and ordinary, life continually encounters messiahs among the things and beings, like a straw amid billions of golden needles.

Living, inert, the things of the world emerge and recount their strange advents. You find these short stories everywhere and always in Biogea; it is enough to bend down and pick them up. The world recounts the contingency of all things, things so similar to us. Atoms incline, collide with each other and make forms, like we do when we caress each other and end up making, unpredictable, unexpected children.

Long time, the world, life, existence or history perhaps don't have any meaning, who knows? Who can know? But these dull courses fill up, at a hundred random crossings, with a thousand imaginable meanings. We live like angels waiting for wonders.

Sadness: does human history invent these mutations when it continually repeats the wars, the violence on women and children, the murders for power, the dull litany of the animal hierarchy asininely imitated by the *sapiens*? Always the same. This history could make a rock cry from boredom and death. How sad that history seems when faced with the crystalline and floral diversity of things; how often human history seems monotonous in comparison to the enchanting adventures of the world. The private short stories of encounters run away from the public hell of power and glory. The planets, species, make love … encounters which move the Sun and the other stars.

And melts the ice in the mountains. Even though it's within a hair's breadth of six thousand meters, Cotopaxi can be climbed without any difficulty; an easy stroll takes you to a beautiful snow-capped cone, Kilimanjaro-style, a final rampart, a bit abrupt, that I wouldn't have known how to surmount without a guide. At the base of the cone, a mountain hut. And then, there I was blocked by a storm. What to do? We tried to leave several times; the snow was whistling sideways; impossible to stand up, zero visibility, hands and nose quickly frozen. Best not tempt the devil.

Stopped by the bad weather, motionless and waiting, I don't get out of my sleeping bag. To the left of my bed, an elderly Englishman, whose heavy melancholy radiated several meters around him. To my right, a slender German woman, athletic, attentive, the very profile of the tireless mountaineer. Law of the mountain: silence, rest, mutual respect. But, after long hours of waiting in bitter cold, you chat. Everyone tells a little about themselves. It warms you up.

A geographer, she claimed that we were close to the summit of the world. We laughed with doubt. Serious, she said that Everest only surpasses the Ecuadorian volcanoes because the usual measure refers to sea level; but if, more precisely, you count the height of the relief in relation to the center of the Earth, Chimborazo, our neighbor wins out over all the others, and our Cotopaxi with it. We took pride in the fact that Ulrike had changed reference points and taken advantage of the bulge in the middle of the planet. The power of her calculations: lying down, we had surpassed Hillary's exploits.

I told them about our two guides and my amazement at having had, for the first time, to choose, at the bottom, at the departure office, between a right-hander, as well as footer, and a left-hander. I jumped at the occasion, which rarely presents itself, of climbing behind a rope leader lateralized like me. At long last, I was going to be able to freely unleash my genetic left-handedness. A disaster! Adapted, since I write with my right hand, therefore completed, even over-adapted for as many decades as is reckoned by my existence to a world where one says straight ahead [*tout droit*] or directly – that is to say, to the right [*droit*] – when one indicates the opposite road, where justice follows the law [*le droit*], that masculine of the straight line [*la droite*], without thinking that, just by saying it, its scales, said to be of fairness, were already leaning to one side, a world, I was saying, where one finds one's bearings by means of a compass, whereas that's already done since one chose the east to be to the right of north.… I suffered through the worst climb of my life. I had hoped to climb to paradise, I continually fell into the subcircles of hell; I thought I was semi-ambidextrous, I was only doubly left-handed; crossing my arms twice for the handholds and my feet for the footholds, and so stumbling and often falling, completely messed up, utterly messed up, I was laughing again at my clumsiness – language says that the lefty is mal-adroit – which amazed my new friends, hearing a story that revealed a minority of which they were unaware, they, being the dominant right-handers, as one says dominant males for elk and sea lions. The hierarchy is blind to minorities. I sing off-key. I walk clumsily [*gauche*]. I suffer from bilateral vertigo.

Ulrike, on my right, laughed, but David, on the left, remained somber. But since, although very poor, my English was better than my German, I had a stronger connection with my male neighbor than my female one, however lively the company of the young woman would have been. Does language draw together more than sex does? And hunger, cold, discomfort, a little anxiety as well before the cone to be conquered in the strong wind made sharing confidences easier.

"Bad news," the gloomy Oxonian confided to me, "my wife is arriving at the end of the week. I haven't seen her for twelve full months; I've devoted my sabbatical year to South and Central America. Paradise. The beauty of the sites, the Latin churches, the Argentine Pampas, the Andean Indians, Iguazu Falls, the Brazilian festivals, the samba, the soccer, the lakes, the Atacama Desert, Bolivia, especially Bolivia … yes, the most beautiful months of my life … culture, that." With the enthusiasm that caught him again, he cheered up. "Alas," he repeated, become gloomy, "my wife is arriving Sunday. She's berating me to take up my old bitch of an existence again. Schedules, appointments, faxes and telephones, only encounters that are prepared, assumed, anesthetized, aseptic, formatted like a newspaper page or a television screen, always the same day, spent in the company of haggard clones, mesmerized by money, power and glory.... Hell, bullshit! Lack of culture, that."

And then, Ulrike, on the right: "Pardon me, I also understand English. I've just learned that the two keepers of the hut have come to the end of their contracts and are looking for replacements. I can become a respectable guide. And you, David? Do you know how to cook? Would you like to stay here for a while with me? The night is falling...."

The storm not abating, I had to go back down to the valley. The couple stayed, here, at five thousand five hundred meters. David also became, I've been told, a respectable guide, while Ulrike started, in turn, excelling in roasts and mashed potatoes. And then, the eruptions of Cotopaxi? Hell? There haven't been any serious ones since 1877.

Encountering, sometimes; being encountered, rarely; playing go-between in an encounter ... but bees play this role for the pollination of plants, without which we would die of hunger; without ten catalysts, absolutely inert, a thousand chemical reactions couldn't take place; more and better, we live thanks to those chemical reactions which require enzymes that are trillions and trillions of times faster and more effective. More parasitical species exist than non-parasitical ones, in Biogea as in every nation. So humans are not the only ones to encounter each other for better or for worse, nor to become messengers: pimps in the underworld of sex, angels for heavenly loves, ambidexters comfortable on both sides. Once again, we're not so original.

Worse: yes, the "counter" of "encounter" often signifies impact, collision, commotion, therefore death. Better: how to make this encounter fertile?

Again a good short story, the briefest of all: some child is cured of meningitis, fatal not long ago. Victory. Recent and sudden, that recovery requires sixty years of hindsight; if some dose of penicillin has just killed, here and now, some bacterium responsible for the disease, it's because some biochemist of genius, in some laboratory, discovered that molecule several decades ago. A troop of beneficiaries ensued, among which was that child, who could be mine or yours. Nothing new under the sun of that true victory, whose entire newness flows back to one proper name, that of the discoverer's. The single short story of the recovering repeats three short stories, like a refrain: let's sing of the sick child, victorious and come out of the hospital this morning; let's honor the memory of Fleming, living and victorious more than a half-century ago; but let's also remember the defeated microbe, present on the Earth for several billion years. Three short stories, three times. Suspense: who is going to win? Who is going to kill the other?

For this single-celled organism, prevented from causing harm by recent human intelligence here and now, appeared on the bacterial Earth, in the midst of thousands of billions of its ancestors forming scarlet pools under a hydrogenated sky, in immemorial times. Mutating with a wild astuteness, it had to adapt itself millions of times to as many good and bad circumstances, worse, to catastrophes we know about, during which, five to six times, more than eighty percent of living beings vanished. Digression: do you know a single short story that's longer, more extraordinary, captivating, moving, cut across with more terrifying suspense than these five or six ruptures during which life, defeated, almost vanished from the Earth? What coups de théâtre! This microbe, yes, the one we're hunting, has withstood countless vicissitudes over an interminable duration. It's thick-skinned. And us, in comparison, how old are we? Not the beloved child, nor Alexander Fleming, nor you or me of course, but Homo, our genus on two legs? Four million years … some hundreds of thousands? That's a handsome young man, this bipedal hominin, so very young, with soft skin, frail, a freshman of life. A crushing comparison with the duration of the microbe's life: several billion against several million, a little first letter of difference. For said bacterium, one of the obstacles scattered in front of it among the enormous sum of those it has known here and now, facing our antibiotics, combated and defeated over more than a colossal duration of time. Will it survive, victorious once again, that umpteenth encounter? Yes, we know, it's already mutating, resisting our weapons. And us, are we mutating? Do we have the time? In this battle, the old don't necessarily lose to the young. For mutation and selection boldly cut down among the most recent. Brief, happy, the short story of the recovery, the one, magnificent, of the discovery, cadence the great, the immense short story of this life, small in size and colossal in duration, like refrains or ritornelli.

Refrain then. Excellent in tactics, our science has just won, for the past half-century, the antibiotic battle; will it find some strategy for winning the war whose long evolutionary course is indeed measured in millions and billions of years? Do we have the time to wait? A crushing comparison between Darwinian time and the short tactics of medical techno-science. In this connection, here's another good short story: our science gains us time. Does not our thought, our discoveries, our knowledge, all staggeringly-fast, move at a speed comparable to that of light? Will the knowledge-hare, at kilometers per second, catch up with the life-tortoise, long and slow? The true war, long-term, is waged between the immense time of evolution and that, luminous, of knowledge: of the two runners, invention and life, which will win out? The rapidity of inventive thought or the patience of the living thing, slow granted, but also sometimes endowed with lightning-fast mutations? For these microbes sometimes prove themselves to be formidably lively and adaptive. There lies the question: how to judge this final sprint? I don't have the time to write this short story, nor the perspicacity to evaluate its outcome. Supposing that we lose this race, will we see the eradication of *sapiens*? What suspense! Worse than a fall, the end?

While awaiting this outcome, undecidable, I'll ask, but for the last time, the question: who is going to win out in the race between mutation and invention, between life and knowledge? Us? The bacteria, our rivals, our adversaries, our enemies? Enduring hatred. Doesn't the recovery of the child – love and paradise – cover up the hellish hate – annihilate the microbe – that we carry in our theoretical knowledge, our practices and our technologies toward what surrounds us – the inert world, living things and fellow humans – toward the entire Biogea? Toward, no, for here is the counter of encounter. Victory, always, against the enemy. Western man, an animal full of hatred? A hatred that makes us think that debate, polemic and combat further things; that hell is others. Us, subjects, have we invented objects so as to better despise them, defeat them, dominate them, hate them? Wasn't old Empedocles right, on the rim of Mount Etna?

And then … far from continually repeating the same question, the same refrain, my new finale reverses the very organization of this challenge: who is going to win? Who is going to kill who or what? For the evolution of life, the immense patience of time makes it probable that chance will turn in favor of the microbe. Since we were talking about war, the old have always killed the young in them; the old men even declare it for that reason. At the end of every accounting, this competition is as dangerous for us as a suicide attempt by Russian roulette.

So, I propose considering the other, wholly other, the other humans, but also every being in the Biogea, neither as rivals in a race that the human animal wins but is going to end by losing, nor as enemies in battle, but as symbionts or mutualists: no more war to the death, rather exchanges of reciprocal services. How can the *against* change into *for* or *with*? How can the current, descending inevitably downstream, in part go back upstream? By following a new time for our refrains, eddies and ritornelli.

Fifth Meditation on our Ways of Knowing and Acting

And so, instead of always seeking temporary victories that can quickly be overturned into definitive defeats, instead of wanting to kill this rival microbe that, mutating as many times as necessary, will almost certainly kill ten great-grandsons of the child recently cured, I'd rather try to decipher its language: the signals that it emits, that it stores, processes and receives, since – it as well as me – we give ourselves over to these four operations. To attempt to open talks with it and negotiate together, thanks to the codes shared in this way, a mutual aid and benefit pact, so that we can pass from parasitism to symbiosis together. That's why I want to listen to the voices of the Biogea while comparing them with ours. Communication, interferences, translation, distribution, passages and bridges. How can the invasive order become a reciprocal dialogue? How can the object become subject? In what language does this mute world speak?

After such an alliance between us, lion, and the single-celled organism, gnat, the female and the male, the sister and the brother, the son and the father would also do so, and thus would the stranger behave toward the natural, the traveler and the native, humans with the living things and, reciprocally, the inert world for the living things and these latter in the first. We would make a common home in Biogea. Where the against would feed the with in return. If we calmed these intentions and these images of combat, our science would change. I want to draw up this peace treaty, this pact, at least, of symbiosis. I've been calling it the Natural Contract for a long time. It has become here the foundation of knowledge, practice and industry.

We aren't the only ones to write and read, to code, to decipher the codes of others, to get decoded by others, to understand, mutate, invent, communicate, exchange signals, process information, encounter one another … to thus win our lives. Everything in the world does it, like us: the light, the wind, the rain, chemical reactions and the reactions of living things, the yews and the sperm whales. The world resonates with a common language, no doubt formal, I don't know if it's poetic but what does it matter, the essential thing remains sharing these codings, this universal language, music and science.

Through deciphering, better and better, these codes attached to things, I can imagine what language this pact could be drawn up in. Information and its codes, as specific and distinguished as the barcodes on our merchandise, together form the language of the world, emitted, received, stored, processed by all things, inert, living, social, you and me included. I swear to compose this new finale one day in that language, in the dialect of the things themselves: in Biogean! Re-birth, co-birth, new behaviors.

Thus will my final short story be written, the one I've wanted to recount since, a glimmer, I've known like the light, since, a fish, I've swum smoothly and supplely like Garonne, since, a porpoise, I've danced like the sea in a beautiful breeze, since, a chamois, I've squeezed the rocky flesh of the cliffs with my hands, since I've mixed my wolf howls with the moans of women and caressed the gentle leaves of the linden with my quivering branches. I'm abandoning the objects, the others, the Underworld, the fights for appalling glories that claim they create the time of history, that grand guignol of blood and tears.

Across the long and empty time, perhaps deprived of meaning, ever since millions of new singular existences emerged, existences dense, for their part, with meaning, galaxies, black holes, planets, bacteria, rats, wolves, jackals, apple trees, oak and linden, *sapiens* ... unforeseeable existences, for all the above, it has been a question of variation of accent, of meaning, of codes, of notes, of syntax, of grammar, of music, of translation on and among this global language, among the infinite of its variants. *Velo* or love, *pompe* or *pompe*, it isn't the same code, it isn't the same thing, some signal displacement.

How can a declaration of open war be translated into a pact or contract? How does the parasite mutate into a symbiont? When will the same animal, killer, decide to cohabitate?

AGAINST

I started my professional life as an assistant to a teacher whose knowledge I respected, from a distance, a knowledge that others, more mediocre still, lacked. He used to invite me to dine with him. On holidays and Sundays, he would buy three cakes, one for his wife, another for him and the last for his two children, a girl and a boy. At the end of the meal, he would dictate: "Fight. The winner will be entitled to the dessert." Powerless, I witnessed this repugnant torture, this maelstrom in which blood would sometimes spurt and in which the father took pleasure, as a profound pedagogue. Later, these two little animals, so correctly trained, would succeed well enough in society. Was I dining at the table of a sage or a wolf?

Ever since, I haven't been able to see a winner's triumph without my stomach turning with nausea, without my mind, astonished at the paltry prizes thus acquired, filling with contempt. Who did that animal kill, and for what cream cake? What stake authorizes these violations, these thefts, this violence? Every fight for a post, for money, a medal, a citation, success, conquest, power, glory casts the combatants down to the rank of those poor brought-to-heel siblings or of bleeding male mammals in combat during the spring for the possession of seemingly submissive females.

The ignominy of the collective is measured by its religion of bestial dominance, by its cult of winners. The skeletons of the defeated harden the steel of their statues.

WITH

In the high mountains, my guide taught me the comfortable cold. "If you curl up into a ball," he said, "if you defend yourself and get dressed, the enemy will penetrate down to your liver: cold is more invasive than you. No. Present yourself, uncover yourself, go toward it, make it your friend; it'll respect you. Turn the *against* into a *for*." Yet without going beyond the lethal limit.

"Dive into the sea or a river. If you splash about and struggle against the water, it'll smother you, drown you. No. Turn the *outside* into an *in*. Make the water your friend, what animates you, and it'll carry you, caress you; you won't ever be able to leave it. A fish. Climb the rock face. If you become frightened against the vertical gravity, it'll hurl you down, push you into the void; you'll fall. No. Turn the *against* into a *with*. Caress the rock like a mistress, and it'll help you and offer you holds; light-heartedly, you will climb it. A chamois. Fly in the air, go gliding or windsurfing, delta-wing or kite. A bird."

Air fills the thorax; ten liquids circulate through the vessels and pores; fire sets the heart, the genitals and the brain ablaze; the humus models the human. How can we live without or against the four elements, without thinking like them, without turning toward them, into them, through them, for them, with them?

With the other humans: the worst dragons of our lives sometimes turn into princesses calling for help. The beast transforms into the beauty: by what trick?

EDDIES: AFTER, BEFORE AND NOW

This one. Avenues of eddies form under bridges, after their piles, where the current runs with the counter-current. The upstream Garonne cascades into the chain of turbulence and leaves it, downstream, just as quickly, but a few circles remain almost stable, the waters of after going back up toward the before, the outside waters entering and leaving, the for and the against mixing, all of it in seemingly motionless cycles in the unstable flames of the flow. It passes and, there, doesn't pass. It seems to produce some now.

Transposed, the same scene happens in the waiting room of a station or any airport in the world. Husky, imposing, sometimes gently seductive, a voice from time to time calls out: Bordeaux, Guéret, Briançon … Turin, Düsseldorf, Sydney, Osaka…. Who has never found themselves stuck in one or the other of these gloomy rooms due to a delay, breakdown, strike, sometimes bad weather? Impossible, for anyone temporarily, to continue the journey. Randomly, passengers arrive, sit down, while certain others leave again. The repair of the breakdown or calming of the thunderstorm might occur in ten seconds, three hours or two days. Waiting: nothing worth telling, nothing happens, except the passing of time. Obeying the voice and as though driven or attracted by it, packets of travelers flow from here, from there, while others flee toward some destination or other. This forms an eddy in which an equivalent or variable number of people - the same, diverse - remain here, seated, lying, eating, conversing or yawning. Entering or leaving, as with the water of Garonne. The kids bawl, the mothers rock them, the men get up, act self-important, carry the suitcases, check the tickets. The luggage follows and imitates the bipeds; green and red volumes of cardboard or leather, fastened tightly or overflowing, appear, are unpacked, pile up. The strident sounds of zippers accompanies the worried questions about changing schedules. The eddy is sometimes formed by the almost circular arrangement of the seats. Never the same men or the same things, always almost the same number.

There, we don't see the microbes pass in transit, the microbes that nonetheless everyone carries by the billions. Here, I don't see my cells change. Yet, they commit suicide by apoptosis every second, new ones replacing them. Am I no longer me? Am I still me? I'm not a substance; I'm an interchange of substitutions. Have I ever seen my wrinkles deepen? My body, every organism – an ontogenetic clock – turns, waltzes and rolls like an eddy. The inert river, airport or station, group, me, the body of every living thing, all of them are images of a certain permanence in the fluctuations of a current. Every existence thus shows something stable in divergence from stability.

A brisk current of arrivals, of births, of replacements, a brisk flight of the dead and of separations that leave circles of population relatively unchanged by these changes. So, phylogenetic, a family, a region, a nation, humanity, all eddy. As with me or my body, a proper name is given to these without caring about just who substitutes for whom, as corpses or newborns, every day, every minute. And yet, it turns! People and groups eddy like the current of the river and of time. Personal or collective, life survives in the quasi stable circles in the flaming current of duration. Where others become same, where the same become other.

Thus, light-years away, coruscant spiral galaxies sow the Universe, a word that signifies *verto*: that it turns; *vers* [toward]: that it goes; *uni*: that it shows stable enough unities. Therefore, this sowing by gigantic spinning worlds gives it its meaning. Closer, all around our globe, anticyclones whirl, in a changeable way, but practically stable. Quartermaster, if you want to survive a deadly cyclone, continue steering your ship within the eye of the storm, just below the maneuvering semi-circle, relatively less knocked about among the hundred gusts that threaten you with shipwreck.

Again, and returning to the living, here are the species that are swept along, formed, mutant, stable and unstable, emergent, put to death by the river Evolution: bacteria, mollusks, fish, insects, saurians, mammals ... never the same, always the same, similar to turbulence. I now know why I'm so fascinated by mollusks, bivalves, tritons, spindle snails, whelks, nautiluses or turbinellas: their windings. Even rocks, even clocks, even time, where the past hurls its waters toward those of the future by eddying around a fleeing present, quasi circular, always there, as though eternal. I take some of that water in my palm and say: now - for the quasi uncapturable instant that I am trying to hold in my hand. And I only succeed at it if the instant eddies.

Fascinated by the death throes of the red cockroaches and the rebirth of the black ones, I see how I managed to forget to relate the opening of the Suez Canal. Not the political one, whose agreement I pathetically negotiated, but the true one: its first filling. I wasn't there of course; I don't even know the story, but a true Gascon knows how to recount things with even more striking and precise details than if he had truly witnessed the event.

Thousands of workers finished, that morning, digging the two sections of the canal, ending at the two Bitter Lakes, located almost in the middle of the isthmus. They lined the bottom of the channel with pozzolana taken from Santorini. At noon, Ferdinand de Lesseps ordered by semaphore the opening of the south and north sluice gates. Brisk, the waters of the Red Sea rushed toward the little lake; muddy, those of the Mediterranean descended in torrents toward the big one. Encounters in Gea: a mixture of tropical liquid and temperate fluid, plus their salinity and a thousand crystals in solution. The two tsunamis face to face caused a giant maelstrom. I would have liked to have seen the furious vortex engendered by those fearsome waves and heard the musical phrase of the successive waves that, in vibration, followed them. Just as Aphrodite was born from a whirlpool of mother waters, so an ocean common to the Atlantic and the Indian came into the world. Through this turbulent birth canal.

Now each of these deluges carried in its mass argonauts and squid, basking and hammerhead sharks, blue fin tuna, dolphins and porpoises, octopi, blower whales, crabs and lobsters, bass and turbots, seaweed, plankton, jellyfish, starfish, turritellas, delphinulas, whelks, columbellas, even sardines; I don't have the time to count the billions of single-celled organisms. Encounters in Bio. I'm not cheating by citing these fish, mollusks, thallophytes, wrack, bacteria and vibrios since even the witnesses who observed the event didn't see these species go by.

Has anyone ever witnessed, ever since God himself populated, they say, the oceans or ever since, they also say, life was born in the deep trenches in the vicinity of submarine volcanoes, has anyone, I was saying, ever witnessed similar nuptials? Did Lesseps dream that he was facilitating millions of affairs, intrigues and philanderings, marriages and cohabitations, hybrids and crossbreedings, legitimate weddings and shady liaisons? Of course, they ate one another a little, a lot, passionately, but strength must be gathered in order to make love madly.

Whirlpools in Gea, intoxications in Bio, a thousand rebirths through the voluble opening of their mixture.

I sing these strong and fragile turbulences – inert, living and human, universal – in rondos, refrains, reprises, ritornelli, waltzes, ballades and barcarolles. Ten forms of narrative, poetry and music whirl in the same fashion, as if these canals and rivers, these cellular elements, life, the rotation of the stars and of atmospheric phenomena, as if the collectives, human and living, time and the nuclear fires of the world, as if I was seeking to envelop them, to develop them with language, with the voice or, better, with the quarter or whole notes launched by Chopin in the Étude whose whirlwind opens his Opus 25.

I take advantage of this opportunity to say and loudly declare that abstract painting, cubes, tears, architecture that's stiff, austere, translucent, linear, sculpture that's geometric or that, sharp, rips bodies to pieces ... formerly corresponded to the sad and puritan boredom, to the high cost, to the devastating cruelty of the old paradigm dominated by the objective, inflexible, rigid, rigorous, cutting, precise, exact, abstract hard sciences which therefore threw the objects at a distance ... mathematics, mechanics, physics ... whereas the new one, centered around the life and Earth sciences, will give birth, like my entire book – crowned with indefinite cycles in its conclusion that waltzes with rolling – to a new aesthetics: one that's marine, land, air, burning, living, plant, floral, fertile, leafy, bushy, exuberant, animal, female, faunlike, fecund, bifurcating, proliferating, seasonal, womblike, diverse, composite, disparate, fragrant, winey, singing, dancing, enthusiastic, animated, whirling ... in love and human. I will see, tomorrow, painters, architects, designers and sculptors, ceramists, filmmakers ... I will hear, tomorrow, poets and musicians ... celebrate, while bursting into laughter, the fertile humus and the opportune life of the Biogea.

I take advantage of this opportunity to say and loudly declare that we will soon witness a reversal of the same order in the technologies and industries. At the beginning of the 19th century, the industrial revolution often resulted in the coupling of the sciences said to be hard and a hundred innovative applications. Comfort and progress of every order came from that once long time happy association, but today it has become progressively outmoded and sometimes dangerous for both humans and the world. Little by little, technologies are decoupling from that old tie to come and couple again with the life and Earth sciences, from now on in central place. A new industrial revolution is being prepared; financial investments are now preferentially going to the biotechnologies, for instance, which were also among the first technologies to come into being – for two narratives of the Flood attest the brewing of beer in the Indian version and, in the Semitic version, wine-making by the patriarch Noah. The upstream of this book returns downstream. Again a refrain, again a turbulence, again a rebirth.

Aquatic vortices, in the sea or a river, tropical cyclones, spiral galaxies, living vertigos of species and organisms, turbulences of large collective populations, aesthetic forms, life … this is an immense vertical cross-section of my short stories or my hymns and the real of the Universe. Closed like stable circles but open to the contingency of chance, recruiting en masse upstream while letting just as strong multiplicities escape downstream, turbulences and barcarolles combine in glory the tumultuous torrent of human vicissitudes and the metamorphoses of the things in the world with the dull repetition of customs and inertias, with the perenniality, immediate and paradisiacal, of luminous concepts and of the love that throws lovers into their rolling bed … that is, certainly, a wide cross-section of the real as such, but also and above all the model, common to all things, big and small, inert, living, reasonable or singing, of evolution, history, time, of every interesting narrative. The model: linear, yes, like an avenue of circles in a laminar flow; cyclic, yes, partially fed by return; chaotic, yes, continuously watered with a very large number of uncertainties, but regulated as future perfect; stable and unstable, yes, in sum eddying, for nourished, in rain, by the upstream and, against the current, by the downstream returned, in part, upstream; therefore by the before, but where a certain *after* flows back and again becomes the *before*; where the *outside* enters and becomes the *in* that, in turn, and partially, goes out.… So, through and across the fleeing flow, I can, a little, hold in my hand the time of now.… It's not so mysterious, it's not so impossible then that the *against* comes back as *with* or as *for*, since it's a question here of a universal dynamics, of a form spread everywhere, of an easy to think model, of quasi necessary narratives … dynamics, form, model, thought, idle tales … in which rational repetition mixes with the contingency of chance. Uncertainties irresistibly rain on the linear falls and metastable cycles. The flowing slipknots of being are born in becoming.

And eddying with joy in the customary misfortunes.

Swirlings: Inside, Outside

I had a sort of scuttle built into the roof, like a crystal ball, even though that year had a swirling spring, the likes of which I hadn't seen for a long time, and of a voluble inconstancy. Beneath the new glass roof I saw, as though I were lying outside, crows, sparrows and turtledoves flitting about left and right, the branches of the maple and poplar twisting, the wind rending the clouds in which tatters of blue passed by in squalls. I already heard the lark singing. There I was given over to the pure turbulence that entered – immense and by its vibrating point – my home and me. Only the rapid fluctuations of warm and cold didn't penetrate beneath the glass of my roof-telescope. The interior had vanished. Conversely, my minuscule and inmost soul freed itself from its turmoils to explode toward these swirlings, outside.

That abrupt exit, I lived it, I knew it by body: the eyes, hands, nose, genitals … launched toward the changing world and the caprice, sometimes torturing, of others a flesh left in the shadow. I also thought that a house imitated the body, dark inside and light toward the outside; but a frail candle or a loved lady-friend illuminates the house's intimacy; a bouquet of lilacs sometimes fills it with its aroma. Black body, white house. No. Transparent, my new crystal ball floods my dwelling and my senses with light. The one entirely outside and the others bright within. It throws me into this churning springtime. The sun breeze, the mixed azure and gray, the liquidness of the sap and the swaying of the trunks, seizing the edges of things with velocity under the breaking up of the rain, mix the evolutionary water, the turbulent air, the winged living things and the intermittent light, amid the round drumming of the background noise. The high washing of the early season.

Proliferating, distributed, profuse, in phase transition, the soul of the world penetrates, in springtime, the shimmering, disparate multiplicities of its body. Thus crying, cheerful, flooded with sobs, furrowed with laughter, my spring body sows my unstable soul with a thousand undulating mixtures. Both swirling, the world and I, we connect, in helices screwed into one another, at the window's opening.

One day, before the Alp, around La Bonette, I had said: there is my soul. This word left my mouth without my wanting it to. Through an aperture of acute suffering, my soul gushed out like a burning geyser and its joy spread spiraling into the space of the col. Ever since my body, instead of contemplating the ceiling, began receiving the sky where, amid the sudden downpours in whirlwinds, the turtledoves were churning the air with their wings above the poplars whose tops were swaying in the wind, my chest has been widening all the way to the clouds that were passing and has been rent with tears or been dissolved by the clouds, in the clouds, with the clouds. I contemplate the soul of the world which contemplates me; I penetrate into this soul which penetrates into me; I sing for it which sings in me; I leave me who descends from it. I think like it.

Without weighing what I was saying, I was estimating, in the mountains, the immensity of a volume, its size; I was leaving my old soul, the small one, the faint-hearted one; I was leaving bias, calculation by pieces, the suffering whose tatters spitefully tear time, finally the evil tied to these details. I was suffering, I will die from the partial that separates. I was attaining a sum that redeems the change. Mixed with the perfection of the Universe, my new soul no longer has any size or age. As immense as space, it lasts, soft, more than duration. Will I know one day whether I have two souls, the narrow one and the large one, the sorrowful one, mortal, and the joyous one, without end, mine, inmost, minuscule, and another, grandiose, attached to the world? Or simply, a single one, contracted, dilated, falling, often, into the rocky time of misfortune, but rising, sometimes, wheeling around the nappe of a cone widening to infinity, to fly, unitive, close to the treeline and the mountaintops, in the turbulence of the wind?

Everything is joy. The elation flies and swims off the coast of everything. I sing my soul that expands, as large as that of the Biogea joy.

Swirlings: Against and With

Why speak incessantly of swirlings, eddies and whirlwinds? Because of the oxymoron, that rhetorical figure where the adjective says exactly the opposite of the noun. *Oxy*: sharp, wily; *moron*: dulled, stupid. Oxymoron: in the literal sense, flat point; in the figurative, subtle simpleton. Here's a poetic example: "*dark light* that falls from the stars"; another, amusing: *military music*; a third, severe and objective: *cultural television*; others, more revealing: *social hierarchy*, the originary and only authentic one remaining the animal one; in *national identity* the adjective designates belonging to a collective and the noun an individual person.... And here's the one that interests me: *sustainable development*, with which everyone today puffs themselves up without ever defining it. Development: evolution; sustainable: quasi-stability in the course of duration. A kind of stop in motion. Oxymoron, contradiction? Those who use this fashionable expression – which would have formerly been called dialectical – do they, too, show a vacant intelligence?

Not entirely, since, in watching a top, everyone can see that it stands all the straighter for its fast turning, that it stays all the more stable for its moving; the gyroscopic compass is based on this paradox, yes, on this oxymoron, where the against feeds the with; likewise for an eddy, an avenue of turbulence, fed upstream by new waters, from which the same or other flows continually flee downstream, and whose form nonetheless remains, quasi permanent; the same goes for all the models from just now, mechanical, biological, social … of the same whirling form, simultaneously other and the same; DNA, continually subject to mutations that change its elements but whose double helix subsists; an organism that loses thousands of cells by apoptosis and replaces them, except for neurons; child, adolescent, adult, old man, other, I nevertheless remain the same; finally, the waiting rooms, a family, a city, a nation, humanity.… Mathematics christens this paradoxical coherence: invariant across variations, a formula that makes the oxymoron's form rigorous, although still contradictory. I can therefore talk about sustainable development.

Just as I can about time. Whose present always remains present and yet is never the same moment. And if time flows, can I hold it, now, in my hand? Yes, if I plunge my hand into an eddy. Then, far from being contradictory, sustainable development, as dull and common as the model of history just outlined, only tells of the ordinary of duration.

But the adjective "sustainable" worries me: what lasts across time? The expected answer: very hard rocks. Objection: does this hard last? The banks of Garonne cave in; the river carries along tons of fine sand torn atom by atom from the rocks of the Pyrenees or the Massif Central. Duration, in the end, erodes the most resistant mountains; Brahmaputra and Ganges will level the Himalayas. This long wearing away can even serve as a clock. Attacked by the incessant surf of the tides, Brittany's granite littorals are cut out into rags worn out down to the detail. In order for the hard to last a little, the powers of this world pile colossal pyramids onto their skeletons; and still, the pyramids disintegrate. No, the hard doesn't last. In the language of the computer sciences: the hard wears away and doesn't last. I invite you to visit the places where the history of technology is read the best: ship graveyards, railroad yards, downgraded cranes, whose masses border the typewriters and computers of the first and even the more recent generations…. Rusted ironmongery fit for making scrap metal merchants rich.

Let's pass from these iron scraps, hard as dirt, to streaming liquids, water. Let's repeat that time flows, that "under the Mirabeau Bridge, flows the Seine, and our loves…." Having never sailed in fresh waters, the poet, from the height of his bridge and his inspiration, didn't see the eddies or the counter-currents that sometimes went against the barges going downstream. Softer than the solid, this is the liquid. The water of the Seine evaporates, forms clouds; it rains. The water has statistically returned. Yes, contrary to what certain people – stupidly landsman – heedlessly repeat, you can swim ten times in the same river. These enormous eddies, widening those of the piles and bridges to the air of the sky, as soft, for their part, as vapors and thick clouds, as high as the skies, as low as the seas, but as lasting as the weather, describe a perennial stability across strong fluctuations. As long as the Biogea has lasted, not one drop of water has gone missing, whereas the hardest mountains flatten, grain by grain, under the soft force of the drops. Although softer than the hard, the soft water lasts longer than the hard.

Does the soft, then, last? Have we ever seen, as with junked cars, such cemeteries for the soft, for breaths and sounds, music, letters and codes, signs and meaning? Imagine some catastrophe, an aerolith crashing into the Earth: cliffs, mountains, walls, crystals, machines … everything collapses and most of the living species die. Even the paintings of the masters, canvases and frames, even the arms of the *Venus de Milo*, even the head of the *Winged Victory of Samothrace*, defeated by time. Do we really need to imagine this end of the world scenario? No, for the two economic systems known to this day, not taking any account of this world, have only taken a few decades, negligible at the scale of the Biogea, to exhaust the mines, the rivers, the entirety of the available stocks, destroying the seas, polluting the air, laying waste to the Earth, killing, at a lightning-fast pace, the living species, in a word, devouring all the earthly capital, hard, accumulated over millions of years, not without drowning what's left of human cultures under a flood of ugliness; better, said sustainable development serves as deceptive advertising for them to finish the plundering. What is left that's lasting? Yes, the soft. Water lasts longer than earth, air longer than water … signs longer than fire. Here is my theorem in full: *the hard does not last, only the soft lasts.*

Objection, again: not even this soft! The gesticulations of a given famous singer only last three months. And the angry political or media cries? The newspaper of the day, fashion, both go out of fashion, the news quickly becomes outdated.

What is left, then? The softest. I rediscover then the methodical path along which I've been walking. I've been climbing, slowly, from granite to water, from the hardest to the softest, from the sea and rivers to the breeze and wind. More and better, from the hard to the soft, from the recording medium to the code. I have to recount then what was recounted long ago and which therefore lasted: naked, shipwrecked, Ulysses reached, lamentable and imploring, the beach where Nausicaa, elegant, was playing ball with her companions, naked … the loves of the Princess of Clèves … Newton's law, Poincaré's theorems … the slow movement of Mozart's Concerto 21 for piano … Fauré's Requiem … all of them contents whose softness borders on excellence. Objections, still: the sublime cantata is no softer than the commonplace song; the recording media made of parchment, paper, wax or silicon for such *dulcissime* contents would definitely vanish by means of the catastrophe of just now, whose power, hard, blind to genius, doesn't choose. So we must find even softer. Let's climb, let's attempt the summit route.

I was speaking about Homer and Fauré…. Question: where are Chopin's *Etudes,* Opus 25? On some disc, interpreted by some pianist? No, there are so many others of them; they print these recording media every day, and by the dozens. On the score? But without an interpreter, it remains mute and sometimes gets lost, mislaid, torn up, remains unable to be found. In our memories? But they're fallible. Where? I know the museum where I can admire the *Venus de Milo*, hard with marble, or the *Mona Lisa*, taut, stiff on the canvas; but where can I find Fauré's *Requiem*? Where does its original lie? Where? Who can answer this old question of *place*? Might information then be all the more lasting, even immortal, because its breath, lighter than air, because its supreme softness, quasi empty, would be absent?

Denis Diderot called on Sophie Volland, his sweet mistress. She wasn't there; patient, he waited; she didn't come; he had to leave, for business. Then, like a flash of lightning from the immortal sky, the most beautiful love letter ever written by a human lover fell from his quill. Here it is, at least such as my memory, reliable, poor, turbulent, can supply it: "I came; I waited for you; you haven't returned. I have to leave. The night is falling. In the dark, I can't see what I'm writing, I can't even see whether I'm writing. So everywhere you see nothing written, read there that I love you."

Nothing written! The *dulcissime* of the quasi vanished soft, a light wind, burning, a light quill lightly borne by the flames and the ultralight breaths of a burning breeze that's vanished like a bit of steam. Will I from now on read that someone loves me everywhere I see nothing written? Throughout the entire Biogea, nothing is written, everything remains written, lasting. Will I finally be able to develop myself there?

What lasts, in the end? What is hardly current anymore and was called the spiritual, whose literal sense expresses breath and about which, in unforgettable times, it was written from the first words of Genesis that its breath, indeed, eddied over the primal waters of the confusion. The fire of God. So, what is to be said about development? Everything. For, starting from that big bang, infinitely soft and lasting, the entire Universe developed.

Again and always an objection: I see that, soft, information forms the world, and that, not yet written, lasting and no doubt stable, it develops everything. At the punctual summit thus attained, I have just transited from *dulcissime* information to the spiritual. Do I have the right to go past that boundary line, from the nothing of meaning to its plenitude? I don't know from whom I can learn whether I can pass this threshold. From Dante? Love moves us, he says in the final line of *Paradise*, just like the Sun and the stars. From Diderot? Blinded, he also saw that love knows how to cross that threshold.

How to go through this narrow door, difficult and yet within reach?

Answer: in silence. Cities, roads and machines, motors and radios plunge the living, intelligent meaning into a stercoraceous confusion, a meaning we destroy with noise after having produced it. Narcissists, *echoists*, we only listen to languages and human rumblings. Constricted in our noises, we shut ourselves up in our clamors. By splashing about in this foul rubbish of meaning, we appropriate the world. *Malfeasance* applies itself to our sound emissions; I sometimes wonder if this invasive invasion of our voices might not thunder like an origin of language.

Thus we only like our oldest short stories, we're only interested in ourselves and our properties. Never in others. I'm not only talking about other ourselves, those who, resonating with languages said to be foreign, nevertheless buzz with human languages. But other *others*: belling or howling living things and resonating things. Yet we're beginning to decipher the codes of living things – true living languages, authentically foreign – and the inert things of the Earth, both of which, like us, receive, transmit, store and process information. Formerly philosophers understood that everything conspires or consents. We now know that the Biogea converses. Scientific or imagined, my brief short stories have tried to make the foreignness, no doubt still unfelt, of these languages heard by building a first megaphone for Gea: seas, rivers, lands, glaciers, volcanoes, winds; then for Bio: rats, wolves and jackals – fauna, apple trees, wisteria, oaks and lindens – flora; lastly by connecting these megaphones to our own encounters and cries. Swirling, the ascent goes from the hell of noise to the smaller and smaller paradise of the said.

At the summit: the non-written or the non-said.

During the night watches, from the zero hour to four, on the Red Sea, on board a broken old tub that was doing three knots – barely the speed of a biped – and from which every evening we saw the green ray, I would organize, on the bridge, against a dangerous sleepiness, short story competitions of every flavor; we heard, precisely, some that were so spicy that I don't dare to tell them here. But when the tears and the laughter died down, the silence of the sea at night took hold of everyone with its magnitude. At the peak of those nights, I myself spoke so frequently of shipwrecks I became convinced that such was my fate. The *Adour*, besides, nearly went down several days later, south of Crete, on Sea Ten. Where the waves thundered with such an intense noise that I thought I heard, once again, behind or under this fearsome fracas, a background of sovereign silence.

For it sometimes happens that the world itself remains silent. The way the love letter to Sophie withdrew into the white. Besides the calm of the tropical sea and the mute hollow of the thunderstorm, these also, peacefully invasive, expand, the muteness of the desert, the voluminous tranquility of the plain, the horizontal calm, suspended from solitude, the immense space of unheard of peace at high altitude, in the vertigo of the mountains, by parachute, hang glider, sailplane … when the background noise of the world dies out. Monks, my brothers in melancholy, human abandonment and superhuman joy, are silent, like me when my words pass onto the page without a racket. For them, God remains silent, involuted into the taciturnity of the world.

The meaning of our words and the non-meaning of things fly – weightless – in relation to what – heavy, immense – is carried by this silence. Its magnificence contains every possible meaning and possible non-meaning, a transparent strongbox for every treasure. No sound, no sign, nothing written nor said … here is, abyssal, the totality of meaning. The meaning of the living and the non-meaning of things converge in the muteness of the world; this meaning and non-meaning plunge there and come out, the ultimate eddy. *Mundus patet*: through a fissure, through an opening, a fault, a cleft come noises, calls as small as these apertures. I'm listening, attentive, I'm translating, I'm advancing in the scaled-down meaning and science. *Mundus patet*: should the world open greatly, it will launch me into its silence. The totality remains silent. Knowledge expanded in elation.

White origin of meaning, fountain of joy.

Flood in Refrain

For billions of years, plants and trees, wisteria, apple trees, oaks and lindens have been continually accumulating an enormous reservoir of oxygen in the air, a treasure that the respirators are burning, little by little.

In the same way, but only for millions of years, children, their mothers, their games, those in love, their beauties, old men, their memories, the naïve, the simple, the poor, the strollers, the men and women who accompany them, the high jumpers, pole vaulters and hurdlers, the inventors, with the timid and the intuitive, the artists, even the comics, as well as the women and men I've never seen because they conceal themselves, mute, for laughs, have been accumulating astronomical volumes of joy, unfortunately untapped due to the rare contemporaries who, furiously addicted to diverse social drugs, for this reason and by making the most noise possible, dominate them. Over that interminable era, this stock – deposited in a pocket, as neglected as dark matter, and like it powerfully in the majority – swelled.

Right up until the morning when, during a sudden silence whose magnitude occupied the entire expanse of space, everything broke. A mute big bang. The skin of the pocket had just given way. So, dense, intense, explosive, joy came, from the left, from the right, in high waves, at ground level, in cataracts and rushing tides, like a tsunami. Liquid, it drowned the beaches like the surf, occupied the trenches of the seas; poured from the clouds in torrents and sheets, snow, hail, rain; gushed high, geysers, fountains; fire, volcano, it sculpted the oval shape of the globe, changed its local climates; air, it wrapped the globe with a flying scarf, blew as a moderate breeze; light, it shined like stars and suns, shimmered with the colors of the rainbow and the constellations. Crystalline, adamantine, it set itself up as the basement layer of the rocks. It created.

By bursting its ancient pocket, joy flooded the living, transpierced the skin of the animals, the tree bark, the fish scales, the artichoke leaves, the ermine and marten fur, the nut shells, even the quills on the backs of the porcupines, penetrated, liquid, into the arteries, the veins, the conduits for sap, the bladders; solid, strengthened the bones, the shells and the carapaces, stretched and hardened the muscles; air, inflated the bronchioles and the swim bladders; fire, raised the penises, inflamed the vulvae, made the hearts beat; soft, fired the intuitions and made the languages, fanfares and chimes ring out.

Joy: the matter from which the Biogea is made.

Univocal Publishing
123 North 3rd Street, #202
Minneapolis, MN 55401
www.univocalpublishing.com

ISBN 9781937561086

Jason Wagner, Drew S. Burk
(Editors)
This work was composed in Minion.
All materials were printed and bound
in June 2012 at Univocal's atelier
in Minneapolis, USA.

The paper is Mohawk Via Linen, Pure White.
The letterpress cover was printed
on Lettra Pearl
Both are archival quality and acid-free.